MISS RUTH

The "More Living Life" of Ruth St. Denis

Other books by Walter Terry

THE BALLET COMPANION: *A Popular Guide for the Ballet-Goer*

ISADORA DUNCAN: *Her Life, Her Art, Her Legacy*

ON POINTE! *The Story of Dancing and Dancers on Toe*

BALLET: *A New Guide to the Liveliest Art*

THE DANCE IN AMERICA

STAR PERFORMANCE: *The Story of the World's Great Ballerinas*

Miss Ruth

The "More Living Life" of Ruth St. Denis

By WALTER TERRY

ILLUSTRATED WITH PHOTOGRAPHS

DODD, MEAD & COMPANY, NEW YORK

Published by Dodd, Mead & Company, Inc.
79 Madison Avenue, New York, N.Y. 10016

Distributed in Canada by
McClelland and Stewart Limited, Toronto

Manufactured in the United States of America

First Edition

Library of Congress Cataloging in Publication Data

Terry, Walter.
    Miss Ruth; the "more living life" of Ruth St. Denis. New
York, Dodd, Mead [1969]
xi, 206 p.   illus., ports.   22 cm.   6.95
    1. St. Denis, Ruth, 1880- I. Title
GV1785.S3T4   793.3'2'0924   70-91280 [B]   MARC

Library of Congress   69

ISBN 0-396-08437-0 (pbk.)

ACKNOWLEDGMENTS: Ted Shawn, who provided me with invaluable materials both from his files and from the treasury of over half a century of memories; Brother St. Denis for equally invaluable recollections of his famous sister, from childhood to her death, and for lending me priceless family photographs as well as theatrical pictures of "Miss Ruth"; Dr. Alma Hawkins, Chairman of the Dance Department of the University of California, Los Angeles, for making the arrangements for me to study the recently acquired Ruth St. Denis journals collection of immeasurable historic importance, and the U.C.L.A. library for its most helpful assistance; Genevieve Oswald, curator of the Dance Collection of the Library and Museum of the Performing Arts in New York's Lincoln Center, for access to the

Acknowledgments

great Denishawn Collection; Frank Derbas, photographer, for making superb reproductions of old and faded photographs; Vocha Fiske, who generously wrote down her memories of seeing Ruth St. Denis dance more than sixty years ago; Phoebe Barr, my first (and greatest) dance teacher, for introducing me to the legend of "Miss Ruth" thirty-five years ago; dancers, students, and fans who have exchanged St. Denis anecdotes with me over the years; and to "Miss Ruth" herself for her words of wit and wisdom and for loving me enough to write to me, frequently and voluminously, for the thirty years of our friendship.

ILLUSTRATIONS

Illustrations

Illustrations

MISS RUTH

The "More Living Life" of Ruth St. Denis

CHAPTER I

I'M A faithless wench," said the white-haired old lady, "faithless to the three of them. All my life, I've worshipped the three: the God in heaven, the god of art, and the god of physical love, and I have vacillated, turning first to one and then to the other. Now that I'm almost ninety, I realize that my art must serve the God in heaven. Physical love? That belongs to the past." Then giving her guest a hearty wallop on the back, she added, "But don't believe for a moment that I don't still *think* about it!"

For nearly a century, this New Jersey farm girl, who became one of the great dance stars of all time, was secretly, and sometimes not so secretly, tormented by her wholehearted, but shifting, responses to these three deities. Her autobiography, *Ruth St. Denis: An Unfinished*

Life, published in 1939, attests to this. Her journals, diaries spanning nearly seventy years, reveal the inner battles—emotional, spiritual, intellectual—of a beautiful woman who also happened to be a genius. She adored sex, she served art with passion, she worshipped God, and she kept doing penance to one or the other for faithlessness. It was destined, of course, from the start. The gawky, limber, adventuresome farm girl, in pre-adolescent days, would sit on the branch of a tree, lie in the fields, retreat to the attic to read, ponder on and absorb what she could of three books: Mary Baker Eddy's *Science and Health With Key to the Scriptures* (which she later stressed was written when Mrs. Eddy was Mrs. Glover), Kant's *Critique of Pure Reason* ("I didn't really understand it, but it entered my consciousness"), and Dumas' *Camille.* In the life which lay ahead of her, she would reflect the powerful influences of all three.

Near the close of her life, when she was channeling her dance genius into the creating of dance liturgies for Christian, Jew, Buddhist, Hindu, and the faithful of the world, she did not forget the ecstasy of the body while serving the ecstasy of the spirit. One day, she had left Manhattan in the morning and returned in the late afternoon in time to attend a dinner party and the theater. "Where were you today?" someone asked. "I went to Perth Amboy—it's in what New Yorkers call 'Joisey'—for a very special reason." A dance lecture, we suggested. "No," she said, "it was a pilgrimage that I have not made in many, many years. I went to the place where I was conceived. Where you were born is unimportant. You're born in labor, in pain, in considerable messiness. What is there to celebrate about that? But you are conceived in love, in passion, and in ecstasy. *That* is when it all begins."

Physically, historically, Ruth Dennis was born in Newark, New Jersey. The year was 1877, 1878, 1879, 1880, depending on varying sources of fact, memory, and legend. Ruthie, as she was to be called throughout her childhood, was the first of two children born to Mr. and Mrs. T. E. Dennis. The father, a native of England but an American citizen and a veteran of the Civil War, had been married before and had a son, Tom. Ruthie's mother, born in upstate New York, the youngest of thirteen children, was a graduate of the University of Michigan and had a degree in medicine. Few women, in those days, were practicing physicians; indeed, in later years, St. Denis would recall that she vaguely remembered her mother telling her that she was one of the first licensed women doctors in the United States.

Mrs. Dennis, before her marriage, practiced in a Philadelphia clinic for a time, but the workload proved too much for her and she was forced to give it up and attend a health center with a water cure. Her months of treatment under the supervision of a Dr. Jackson left her with an abiding concern for natural methods of well-being. She never returned to medicine, but focused her interests on health, beauty, and religion, and these profound motivations in her life she passed on to her daughter.

Mr. Dennis, who had obtained a divorce from his first

wife in order to marry the thirty-year-old former doctor, was an inventor and sometime engineer. As a family provider, he left something to be desired, and the child who was to become "The First Lady of American Dance" in the eyes of the world, and "Miss Ruth" in the hearts of dancers around that world, recognized both his brilliance and his weaknesses. She often recalled that he dreamed of flights to the stars in an age when men were "crawling." But she also remembered that in moments of despondence he found solace in "Irish whiskey" and that Old Dan, the horse, would dutifully draw the family carriage back home to the farm after his master's long session in a saloon in Somerville.

It was at Pin Oaks, the farm near Somerville, New Jersey, that Ruthie Dennis grew up, found her gods, and, unknowingly, mirrored in miniature the natures of both parents: religion and dreams, discipline and fancy, aspiration and despair, remorseless drive and self-indulgence, and certainly that quality, that essential of genius which Martha Graham was later to describe as "divine discontent." For Ruthie Dennis not only ran with laughter through the fields, she also emulated the Crucifixion in the secrecy of her room in order to find a physical identity with an event which had rechanneled the rush of history itself.

Still, on the farm, she was an innocent. But it was by no means a bland innocence. She adored to romp with Tige, the bulldog; already there was something of the bulldog in her nature. She loved listening to her mother read the Bible, although she didn't always understand it, but she did understand that pure religion had little to do with Methodist services, which she found "lugubrious." She not only made obeisance to the sun as it set, but it was quite clear to her that Jesus Christ was closer to that sun, to the sea, to all of nature than He was to the church services she abhorred.

Right then and there she began to do battle with orthodoxy. Like her great contemporary, Isadora Duncan, she found inspiration for the movements of dance in nature, in the roll of the sea and the bending of flowers; and in the 1880's, a continent apart, two little girls who were destined to alter the course of dance, of theater, of art itself were dancing with nature, Isadora by the ocean in California; Ruthie by the fields and streams of the old farm. They did more than imitate nature in dance—that was a way of dance as old as man himself— they let nature invade their spirits and in it they found faith as well as art. One of the recurrent poses of Isadora Duncan was with arms open reaching upward toward the sky, and you will find Ruth St. Denis with a single arm raised, pointing toward majestic mountains, to heaven, toward an invisible aspiration.

Years later, when she was world famous, the Christian Science Church was, understandably, proud to claim her as a devoted follower. She was devoted but not, however, abject. She once noted, in Christian Science circles, that there were certain teachings of Buddha that would benefit Christian Science teachings. Indeed, "Miss Ruth" saw no problems in interweaving the tenets and lore and colors of various faiths. It was she herself who pointed out that her historic ballet *Radha* concerned a Hindu goddess dancing a Buddhist concept in a Jain temple!

But how did dancing and religious fervor come together down on the farm? There was no immediate awareness of the linking of the two, but here the seeds were sown. By doing her own Crucifixion, Ruthie, in a very elementary ritual, had sought to identify herself with a profound Passion, and although she did not know it at the time, her "acting out" of this was the start of her lifelong dedication to dance as ritual, as theater. But the act of dancing came first.

While Isadora, at four or five, was waving her arms rhythmically and teaching other little girls and even babies to move in harmonious patterns (this was the first Duncan "school of dancing"!), Ruthie Dennis was displaying her own responses to those stimuli which make all living creatures, birds and animals as well as humans, want to dance. In her autobiography, she describes this with high good humor. She wrote: "An ancient tradition has it that when I was three years old Father, who played the violin and belonged to a little country dance orchestra, took me to a barn dance. As soon as I heard the music—so runs the hoary legend—I began to jounce up and down, and Father, seizing a tambourine from the trap drummer, thrust it into my hands. I started beating out the time, with some uncertain footwork to accompany it, a line of conduct I have followed ever since."

Ruthie, as a child, had no extensive dance training. In later years she always described her dancing as self-taught. But she did, in girlhood, have a few lessons. The formal dance exposures, however, seemed to have little effect on her. She was an instinctive dancer to begin with, and factors which influenced her career were what she saw in the way of highly theatrical stagings (circuses, spectacles, and the like) and the teachings of a man who was neither a dancer nor a choreographer! Ruthie, of course, never studied with François Delsarte himself (1811–71), but she learned first about Delsarte from her mother and subsequently saw performers who were pupils of Delsarte or pupils of pupils. The importance of Delsarte, a successful singer at the Paris Opéra, an artist who lost his voice because of bad training and who turned to studies of the relationship of anatomy and emotion, cannot be overestimated. Not only did his theories, no matter how diluted, guide Ruth St. Denis, they influenced beyond measure the entire structure of American modern dance.

Very recently it was discovered that Isadora had paid tribute to Delsarte and his influence on her in a published article of the 1890's. Many years later Ted Shawn, who became Ruth St. Denis's husband, found important movement roots in Delsarte and ultimately became America's foremost expert on Delsartean principles.

The New Jersey farm girl first learned of Delsarte through her mother, who had known Steele Mackaye, the great actor and disciple of Delsarte, during her association with an arts colony in Perth Amboy, and who later had met a Mme Poté, a distant associate of the Delsarte school. Mrs. Dennis gave Delsarte exercises to her gangling daughter, who had started out in life as a weakling and then, suddenly, had grown too fast. But along with these exercises came driblets of Delsartean principles of meaningful movement. At the time, little Ruthie was aware only of the discipline of the exercises as she swung her long legs in rhythm, straightened her back, moved her long arms. But this was simply Mother's therapy for a growing girl. A few years later, however, Ruthie was to see a performance by Genevieve Stebbins, a Delsarte disciple, and this made an indelible impression on her. For more than seventy years, the images of Stebbins in concert remained clearly etched in her mind. The influence was undeniable, but at the time there was no immediate identity with Delsarte and her own childish explorations of dancing in the sun or dressing up to imitate something or someone.

But so important is Delsarte, so strange is his influence on an alien dance form with which he had no direct contact whatsoever, that a resumé of his findings and teachings is essential to an understanding of American dance of the twentieth century and, certainly, of Ruth St. Denis who, unknowingly, fused brilliant stagecraft, ethnic colors, philosophy, and religions with a concept of movement that was scientifically planned to reveal the true feelings of the inner being.

Delsarte, with a singing voice gone forever, made his life's work a study, exploration, analysis, and codification of gestures which would bring verity to the performances of singers and actors—he knew nothing about dancers. For years he observed the movements of prisoners, of mothers as distinct from nursemaids, of soldiers, of innocents, of sophisticates. He watched pain and ecstasy, despair and exaltation. He then evolved a method, or more accurately, a theory, whereby the actor could dispense with stock gesture and project with honesty, inner feelings. Ironically, he was misunderstood by many, and his "examples" of emotional gesture became "stock."

Delsarte became the rage everywhere. Ted Shawn reports in his book on Delsarte principles, *Every Little Movement,* that such was the vogue of Delsarte that all manner of products carried his name, including corsets and crutches. Ladies with a leaning toward elocution learned superficial gestures and took to the stage, the lecture platform, the drawing room. They, and their ilk, made a mockery of Delsarte, perhaps unconsciously, and it would be left to dance and dancers to rescue this remarkable scientist of movement from ignominy. How much of the principles of Delsarte Mother Dennis got from Mme Poté is debatable; probably very little, for she was concerned mainly with health measures, including regulated, rhythmic exercise. Certainly Ruthie never identified these Delsarte drills with dance, but the first seeds were planted then, to find germination at a later date through the impact that Mme Stebbins had on her and, eventually, through her own need to evolve meaningful movement in dance in an era when dance, in the Western world, was devoid of meaning.

Isadora, from random references in her writings, must have had similar, unwitting, unanalyzed experiences. Only Shawn, scientifically and purposefully, applied

Delsartean principles to dance performance and dance education many, many years later.

Miss Ruth, in the historic, artistically revolutionary dances which were to follow a decade as a show-business dancer, mirrored Delsartean principles, although she was not consciously aware of this until she had met, married, and discussed it with Shawn at a later date.

What were these Delsarte elements which were to be so important to the art of Ruth St. Denis and the generations of dancers who would follow her?

Delsarte, through his years of observation of the movement behavior of man under a wide variety of emotions, conditions, and relationships, divided the body into three basic areas: the lower abdomen was the physical zone; the central part of the body, the torso, was the spiritual zone; and the head comprised the mental zone. The space lying outside these body areas partook of the same classifications and even the limbs were similarly subdivided so that, for example, the heavy upper arms represented physicality; the lower arms, the emotional area; and the hand, the mental part of the arm.

Ruthie Dennis, in the first phase of her career as a professional dancer (1894–1904), was a physical dancer specializing in leg work, in the kicks, splits, and the skirt manipulations popular in vaudeville. When "sainted" into Ruth St. Denis, her dance interest turned to the spiritual area, and many of the images she has left in memory and in photographs are of the arms raised to the spiritual zone above her head. Of course, in her famous nautch dances of the street girls of India, the movement accents were on the feet with their ankle bells and upon the free-moving hips. Even the arms and hands moved mainly in the space zones that Delsarte thought of as physical and emotional. Isadora, once she too had left show business for the dance art she founded, stated that the soul was in "the solar plexus." Spiritually, her questing arms reached upward in one of the gestures so often identified with her.

But neither girl consciously drew deep esthetic purposes from Delsarte. They were exposed to him, no matter how haphazardly and even superficially, and they responded, purely by instinct.

Ruthie, consciously, responded to anything theatrical. At nine, a family friend took her all the way from the farm in Jersey to upper Manhattan, where she saw the Barnum and Bailey Circus. Nothing stuck in her mind except the extravagant finale which was "The Burning of Rome." Here she saw the Christians praying as the fire spread inexorably closer and closer as the music soared to a dramatic climax. Miss Ruth, into her ninetieth year, could describe the scene in detail. As a child, it made an impression which was to influence her whole concept of theater dance, although the spectacle itself was in no sense a dance or a ballet. Only later would she, unique among choreographers, relate this spectacle and its dramatic intent to the art of expressional dance.

Such was the impact of "The Burning of Rome" on the child that when she got back to the farm she got hold of some old curtains and cut them into her very first dance costume.

In preteen-age days, she was also exposed to another spectacle, "Egypt Through the Centuries," which she saw at Palisades Park in New Jersey. It was staged by a very successful dance master of the period, Imra Kiralfy, and Miss Ruth recalled that some of the dancing was done in toe shoes. Later, she would disapprove of such ethnic and period inaccuracies, but at the time, she was deeply affected by the spectacle itself and by the evocation of an antique civilization. The exquisite costumes— all her life, costumes would be paramount in her overall concept of dance theater—and a point of view on life in ancient Egypt made their imprint on an impressionable girl. Twenty years later, she would do a historic ballet, *Egypta*, totally different from the toe-dancing at the Palisades, but closely linked in terms of theater spectacle.

To understand the sudden, unpredictable flowering of a genius who changed not only the course of dance history but theater too, one must sense the tremendous theatrical forces that "The Burning of Rome" and "Egypt Through the Centuries" exerted on a strange and restless child. The third influence was, of course, Delsarte. Here was a trinity, just as there was a trinity in Delsarte's triune division of the body, the limbs, and the space surrounding those areas of action.

In her eighties, Miss Ruth mused on Delsarte "leaning over the golden bar of heaven" and wondering what on earth Mrs. Dennis had taught her lanky daughter, via Mme Poté, about his principles. With Mme Stebbins,

Ruthie was on firmer ground—she saw, she absorbed, she was illuminated.

Before Stebbins, she never actually thought of herself as a dancer—she was simply a little girl with agile limbs and an exuberance which had her running in the sun or dashing out, with a minimum of clothes, into a warm summer shower. When Mrs. Dennis was given a pair of tickets for a recital by Genevieve Stebbins, she took her daughter along. The child was almost overwhelmed by the beauty of the woman, clad in soft material that draped like the garments of classical Greece. Her attitudes seemed to be derived from Greek statues and her gestures stemmed from the laws of Delsarte. Against a background of simple, unadorned curtains, she mimed the role of Niobe, and most important to Ruthie, she performed something called "The Dance of Day," a pattern of movement from dawn to sunset. Many years later, in her *Egypta*, Ruth St. Denis based her creation on the day in the life of an entire nation, from sunrise to sunset, from birth to death.

Seventy years after the child had been exposed to Genevieve Stebbins, memories of her were as sharp and clear as photographs. "I saw her from the balcony of a theater when I was about eleven years old. I think of all the people I have ever seen in my life as far as influencing the very core of me, that the serenity and co-ordination because she, consciously or unconsciously, had much that Isadora had. I wouldn't say that she had quite that exquisite abandon to rhythm. She was a more conservative personality apparently, but when she moved it was like an angel, it was like a goddess. And in all the little vaudeville bits and things I had ever attended, I had never seen anything like her. She had lovely golden hair and when she moved to whatever music—I can't remember—I just know that I said to myself, or rather, my spirit said it, not my brain looking at her, something within me said, 'That is the way I want to dance.' Something was born at that moment."

What little formal training Ruthie had began in Somerville, where she studied social dancing with Maude Davenport. The tree-climbing tomboy who hated school and detested the deadly formality of church took to these lessons, but it was soon clear that her dance needs were more complex, so it was arranged that she have an audition with a New York teacher of dancing, Karl Marwig. Whatever he saw in the lanky, untrained, poorly dressed farm girl, he did recognize a basic talent, and he agreed to teach her.

But the Dennis family had no money for weekly travels to and from New York, so Ruthie earned her fare. She collected watercress from a cool stream, put it in little baskets, and went from house to house selling it for a nickel a basket.

Her dancing, her free spirit, and her rebelliousness against convention shocked her nonconservative mother's conservative relatives. Some of them banded together and raised sufficient funds to send the obstreperous thirteen-year-old to the Dwight Moody Seminary in Northfield, Massachusetts. The association with the famous evangelist didn't last long. When he learned that she planned to take part in some theatricals at home, he lectured her on the immorality of the theater, and she countered by telling him that from her viewpoint he was a narrow-minded old bigot. She fled the Seminary and went home in time to dance in a play called *The Old Homestead.* The dance was, of course, interpolated, and the neighbors referred to it as "Ruthie's Delsarte." Her mother accompanied her on the piano. The occasion was a fund-raising venture for a new school flag, and the performance took place in the red schoolhouse itself. The dance was called "Lessons from Delsarte," for the word "dance" was not in good standing in proper circles. People in the audience, embarrassed by her strange antics, laughed at her, but the play, in which both Mr. and Mrs. Dennis appeared as actors, was successful enough to be moved on to a big hall in Somerville itself. There, Ruthie Dennis earned her first newspaper review. The *Unionist-Gazette* praised the play, applauded Mr. and Mrs. Dennis, and wrote that "Ruthie Dennis was the star of the performance in her skirt dances." The year was 1893.

Mrs. Dennis was the most important being in her daughter's life. It did not mean that she always understood Ruthie, but she accepted her. With equanimity, she accepted the blowup with the Reverend Moody, even though it meant a rift with her relatives. Furthermore, she knew that her daughter was odd, fey, unpredictable, enormously talented, and possibly a genius. She didn't indulge her. She guided her, and she continued to do so until an internationally famous star needed her no more, that is, when she married someone who would indulge her and guide her, Ted Shawn.

But Mother wasn't the only figure in her life. She adored her improvident father, although she battled with him, and much of her own reckless, inspired undiscipline came from him. All her life she would be a wild confluence of the two—the dreams of her father, the dutifulness, if not the practicality, of her mother. But there were others. She liked her half brother, Tom, but she loved and needed (and used, with his consent) her full brother, Buzz. Buzz was eight years her junior. His parents never got around to naming him, so he was first Brother Dennis, then Brother St. Denis, or B. St. Denis. He was destined to play a major role in his sister's career, for he, too, recognized her genius, and with his father's gift for invention, he contrived stage effects which she demanded but could not, herself, produce.

There were also her best friend, Lizzie, who unknowingly made Ruthie terrified of marriage, and her first beau, Clark Miller, the village iceman. On their first date Clark was allowed to pick her up in his horse-drawn sleigh, because her father felt that the boy was "honest," although her mother was worried. In the years to come, Ruthie, tormented and tempest-tossed, looked back and wondered if she shouldn't have married the iceman.

As for Lizzie, her gay, laughing friend, her boon companion, she saw her finally as a young matron, terribly aged before her time, with a baby, with poverty, with a tired husband who wanted to go to bed with her and make more babies. Ruthie took one look and said,

"That's marriage." Twenty years later, when Ruth St. Denis married Ted Shawn, this marital image was still in her mind. She equated marriage and Lizzie and she was terrified at what she saw. So strong was this memory that, in sheer fright of becoming pregnant and turning into another Lizzie, she postponed the consummation of her marriage to Ted Shawn—this was 1914—and according to him, employed every known form of birth control to avoid conception.

But in 1894 this was not a problem. There were, however, two problems: one was how to keep from losing the farm despite the income obtained from summer boarders; the other was to fulfill Ruthie's increasing urge to be a dancer. The farm was lost in 1896, but before that, Ruthie Dennis at sixteen or seventeen had become a professional dancer. And she got her first job in unorthodox fashion. Since theater managers were not interested in seeing an unknown, untrained teenager, she forced the issue by auditioning, unrequested, in the lobby—in front of the ticket booth—of a New York theater. She was hired. The rest is dance history.

CHAPTER II

MOTHER and Ruthie, on this day, made the momentous journey to Manhattan—Mr. Dennis was not at all certain that the stage was the best thing for his daughter—quite certain that Miss Davenport's and Marwig's approval and the enthusiasm of the boarders down on the farm could not be misguided. They knew nothing about the business side of the theater, about managers, agents, bookers, producers, so they started the venture doing the only thing they were sure of: they went to a theater and simply began their campaign.

The theater they picked, on Sixth Avenue, was called Worth's Museum. Actually, it was a combination of a variety house and a monster museum. Even late in life, Miss Ruth would shudder at the memory of pickled monstrosities of nature at which ticket buyers gawked.

After seeing the monsters and the vaudeville act, Mrs. Dennis went up to the ticket man in the box office and stated firmly that her talented daughter would like to dance for him then and there—she had no notion that there was anybody of any greater authority on the premises. Smilingly, he agreed, and little Ruthie, tossing her curls while her mother held her little sailor hat, had her first audition in the foyer of the theater. Since no piano was at hand, she did not do the little dance she had prepared, so she improvised and highlighted it all with the high kicks of which she was inordinately proud. Hers, she often recalled, were unusual in that they were "slow kicks." Most dancers slammed into them, but not Ruthie; she would raise the leg until it gently rested against her face, and then she would reverse the procedure by doing a slow kick to the back of her head. The man in the ticket booth and those passers-by who stopped for a look seemed to approve of the agile, vivacious teenager, and so she was told to return the next morning for a proper audition in the theater for the manager himself. All excited, heartened, and hopeful, they arrived promptly, this time equipped with the music, "Gavotte d'Amour," which the bored accompanist played. This time, in addition to the high kicks, she did backbends, rollovers, and splits (slow splits), and she got the job.

She was expected to give eleven performances a day and her salary was to be twenty dollars per week. In her autobiography, she gives this figure, but occasionally, in subsequent reminiscences, she would say that she received eleven dollars a week for the eleven shows a day.

Certainly, in the ledgers, old and faded, on another variety house, there is an entry which says simply, "Ruthie—$12.00." Whatever she had—skill, youth, charm —she made the grade and she was held over for a second week at Worth's.

"What I did in those first vaudeville years," she recalled, "was really very ordinary. I could copy anyone. Technique? Never heard of it. With me, 'there wan't none!' I'd just look at some of the girls with acrobatic tricks, watch them twice and then do what they did. I really belonged to the 'do-it-yourself' school of dancing. I was like thousands of other girls with lithe, quick bodies, who loved rhythm, who danced easily to whatever music was being played, and somebody told them they could earn a living by it, and so I tried it in vaudeville and in this and that. It was most ordinary, I assure you. Except I'll say this in defense, that it is possible, only possible, that what we today call quality of movement might have been recognized by a dance critic if we had had any in those days. He might have said, 'That girl has something.' Not for what I did but for the way I did it."

Ruthie, in addition to her mother's Delsarte exercises, had a certain coordination of movement which "only the Lord taught me, and no one else," an innate shrewdness which made her realize that her stunts (because they were not as extensive as those of other dancers) had to be delivered with great panache, and an irresistible smile of the lips and eyes.

Still, even in those days, she was not content with

what she was doing. True, she wasn't at all sure just what her goals were, but there was an inner restlessness which kept her on the watch. She would run off-stage after a particularly well-received performance of her cartwheels, kicks, splits, and rollovers, and weep to her mother that if people applauded those silly things they would never applaud what she really had in mind. She did not, of course, have anything in mind at the time—she had something inside herself, something that she put into words in a radio interview when she was nearing ninety: ". . . to dance is the impulse of the spirit. I took an activity and made an art." In the 1890's she had discovered how to use the activities of which her young and supple body was capable, but she had yet to discover how to use that very special body in terms of art. She felt the impulse but she did not know the pathway it should follow.

She even tried classical ballet, for although she was contemptuous of toe-dancing—it seemed unnatural to a farm girl who ran barefoot through the dewy grass—she knew it to be a dance form with a history. She took some lessons from Marie Bonfanti, the retired ballerina who had dazzled New York in the great extravaganza *The Black Crook,* which had opened in 1866 and had run for an unprecedented two years while ministers raged and warned from pulpits and ticket sales soared.

Ruthie did not take to ballet lessons, and apparently Mme Bonfanti did not take to her. In later years, St. Denis, the star, often said, "I learned three of the possible five positions of the feet and was asked to leave." At the same period, and perhaps during the very same days, another teenager destined for fame gave the ballet a try with Mme Bonfanti and decided that classical dancing of that sort was not for her. Her name was Isadora Duncan. Whether the two teenagers expressed joint disgruntlement in the ballet dressing rooms is not known. Certainly they were to become the most celebrated ex-students that Bonfanti, herself a great dancer, ever had.

This was the period of the plump, tightly corseted, female ballet dancer—there were few, if any, *danseurs,* and male ballet roles at the Metropolitan Opera were done by girls *en travesti*—and neither Isadora nor Ruth Dennis approved of such constricting dress. It was partly for this reason that Duncan turned to the light tunic of ancient Greece. Indeed, it was she who was soon to free the modern female from her corsets by the example of her own dress, or undress. Ruthie, as Ruth St. Denis, would not take credit for abolishing the corset, but because of her East Indian costumes, with the bare midriff, she used to joke that she was the mother of the bikini bathing suit and that her costumes symbolized "the separation of church and state!"

Brother St. Denis, in his eighties in 1969, recalled that Mrs. Dennis actually crusaded against corsets in the nineties. She preached against long dresses, because they were unsanitary, and against wasp waists, "and she even used diagrams to show what wasp waists did to the organs. Mother was a forceful woman." Ruthie, understandably, was strongly influenced by her mother's preachments on dress, and her dance dress was similarly affected.

When Ruthie played Worth's Museum and other theaters, she and her mother could not very well commute
from Pin Oaks to Manhattan. They stayed at Miller's
Hotel on Twenty-sixth Street, a small inn owned by a
Mrs. Miller who, with her brother, held the mortgage
on the Dennis farm. It was this mortgage that paid for
enlarging the house so that Mrs. Dennis could take in
a greater number of boarders, a necessary source of income for a rather poor family. The little hotel catered
to artists, and the atmosphere was congenial to Ruthie,
her mother, brother Buzz, and friends. Among these
friends was the Countess Ada de Lachau, an impover-
ished noblewoman who became an esthetic and spiritual
force in the lives of both Mrs. Dennis and her daughter.
"Beloved Ada" was to remain perhaps the closest friend
of the Dennis family for all her life, more than half a
century. It was to Ada that Ruthie turned for help when
she was about to make the break with show-business
dancing and it was to Ada that she turned, in moments
of emotional turmoil, in the decades ahead.

After the Worth's engagement and other vaudeville
appearances, an agent asked her for photographs and
offered to book her. While waiting for results, she and
her mother went back to the farm, as they always did
when not occupied in New York, and Ruthie continued
her schooling, with Mrs. Dennis as her tutor. Then came
the call from the agent—a performance for the Metropolitan Opera Club! Traveling by buggy from the farm
to the station and from there to Manhattan in something
that approached blizzard conditions, she made the event.

She was late, but she danced and successfully. As she ran down a corridor, she bumped into a red-headed gentleman who complimented her. Later, she received a letter from him inviting her to attend a ball with him. His name was Stanford White, famed as an architect and celebrated for his taste in beautiful women. (Ultimately, he was to die by a bullet fired by a jealous gentleman because of a beautiful performer.) Mrs. Dennis knew *both* reputations of Stanford White, but she permitted her daughter to go to the ball. She, however, went along as an eagle-eyed chaperon.

White admired Ruthie and was fond of her. She was treated to flowers and other proper attentions of a beau, but mother would not permit gifts of jewelry. So Stanford White gave his little friend a bicycle. She loved it. She used it to escape by herself into her own dream world and she even used it to earn a living between dance engagements.

At home, matters were at low ebb. Debts piled up and the farm had to go to a new tenant. Household goods were auctioned off, and the Dennis family moved to Brooklyn where Mr. Dennis's son Tom and his wife lived. Both Mother and Ruthie were heartbroken at the loss of their beloved Pin Oaks and they vowed that they would come back to it. Brother remembered that it was a huge white house, changed from a one-time County Poor House into an inviting home, and he also recalled that Mr. Dennis, when the farm was lost, blamed the administration of Grover Cleveland. "Dad always said that business was good before the Cleveland administration and after it took office, business was bad."

But Mr. Dennis was not a very good businessman. Brother St. Denis, devoted to his sister and highly sensitive to her artistic aims, was still very sympathetic to his father, and as it turned out, his own highly successful career would be an admixture of the two totally different personalities. "Mother," he says, "had a business drive. She managed, and well, everything about Ruth's career. Dad wasn't too much interested in what Ruth was doing. Mother, I guess, left Dad somewhere along the wayside as she guided Ruth's career. But Dad was a good toolmaker, a good mechanic in the Brooklyn Navy Yard. As Ruth wrote in her book, he was also a good inventor. He invented many things. I remember that he invented a special kind of speaking tube for battleships, one which wouldn't overheat as the older ones did. But he never did get paid for it—I guess he didn't try to patent it—and he never realized much from his other inventions. I was more businesslike. I, as a boy, used to collect leftover brass at the Navy Yard and sell it for all of three dollars."

Ruthie loathed Brooklyn to begin with, and on top of the sad move from farm to city, things were bad. Dance jobs were sporadic, and the bicycle became a means of escape from a dreary home. For a time, she returned to formal education by attending Packer Institute in Brooklyn, and while there, created and performed a dance in the freestyle movement which, perhaps, characterized the dances of ancient Greece. This took place several years before she saw Isadora dance and simply bears out her theory that inventions along the same lines occur, in science or in art, at the same time in different parts of the world because they are needed and the moment is at hand.

But she had to earn money. So for a brief period she worked as a "cloak model" at Brooklyn's most famous department store, Abraham & Straus, and although she danced in the dressing rooms and flaunted authority as much as she dared, she was a successful model. When family funds, on another occasion, were at a very low ebb, she entered a six-day bicycle race at Madison Square Garden. Her vehicle was, of course, the gift from Stanford White. About halfway through the race, before she had gotten her second wind, she was pumping her pedals at the point of exhaustion, when a burly, red-headed Irishman stepped out from an entryway, lifted her off her bicycle, carried her to a room, and placed her on a table. "This is it," she thought. "This is rape. And I'm too tired to care." It was a masseur. Ruthie came in sixth.

Ruthie wasn't used to coming in behind anyone. Shortly thereafter, she entered another marathon bicycle contest and won the championship.

There were, of course, jobs in the theater at varying intervals. In 1898 she applied for the title part in a show called *The Ballet Girl*. Although the producer knew of her as a skirt dancer and was surprised that she had turned up for a ballet part, she convinced him that she could do the job. She went home to Brooklyn and practiced doing *piqué* turns around the dining-room table.

She knew that her ballet technique was limited, so although she danced on *pointe* for the first and last time in her life, she felt that she must add some sort of fillip to her performance. She ended her ballet routine with a jump over a balustrade to a lower stage level, and landing on her knees, slid as far as she could and did a rollover into a split! Ruthie was a tall girl, a big girl, and her normal weight was about 135 to 140 pounds at her dancing peak. Whether the bicycle races or the knee jumps were to blame, in subsequent years she was destined to suffer from heavy legs (which she concealed brilliantly) and thick knees. In her eighties, she would say, "The knees, dear, have bothered me since 1900; they're just a little worse now."

She could have skipped all the ugliness of Brooklyn, the insecurities of life in the theater by marrying her iceman—he was willing to wait for her, and she returned to Jersey to see him from time to time—or she might possibly have become the mistress of Stanford White. She chose neither. An inexorable drive was there. It was the career. Augustin Daly was next on the Dennis list. The wait was long, but finally Ruthie was hired for a show, *The Runaway Girl.* Daly was the producer-director who was badgered into hiring Isadora Duncan. Neither girl made a major mark under him, although both were paid.

With Daly's death, a continuing association for Ruthie was ended. She was desperate. There were no jobs in the theater. Her hard-working agent finally called. David Belasco, the great director, could use her in a show starring Mrs. Leslie Carter. She had been modeling at Abraham & Straus and was getting a weekly paycheck despite her bad behavior. Could she afford to give this up? Could she leave, almost instantly, for London? Father Dennis disapproved. Mother Dennis said "Yes." It was 1899 and the Belasco years had begun.

CHAPTER III

I'M GOING to keep an eye on you," said the young actor to the young actress on board ship. In truth, he was a deputy for Stanford White, who had promised a worried Mrs. Dennis that he would be going to London soon and would watch out for her there. In the interim, Mark Smith, a member of the Belasco company, had promised to keep the irrepressible, and flirtatious, Ruthie under surveillance.

In *Zaza,* starring Mrs. Carter, Ruthie played the role of a ballet girl, but she did not dance at all, for it was simply a small acting part. Indeed, with Belasco she was an actress, and for most of her five years with him, she rarely danced and hardly ever practiced, "because," as she put it, "I am constitutionally lazy." But her naturally limber body survived the neglect.

The Belasco years had begun April 4, 1900, with the departure of the *St. Paul* to Europe. Once there, rehearsals kept her occupied, and on this first trip to London she had no time to attend English pantomimes, theater events of any sort, including a staging of *A Midsummer Night's Dream* in which another young American girl was enjoying a modest success as one of the attendant fairies, "prettily played by Miss Isadora Duncan." On April 16 *Zaza* opened, but there was no mention of Ruthie except in the cast listing of Ruth Dennis as Adele. Still, Ruthie was excited by the occasion and wrote that *Zaza* was "a big success."

If evening performances of *Zaza* prevented Ruthie from seeing theater events in London, nonmatinee days gave her time to see the sights. In letters home she gave colorful descriptions of everything from the lovely English countryside to the queen. As always, sensitivity and levity intermingled. "I have much to be thankful for," she wrote, "and one thing is that Lydia Pinkham, the kind you have always bought, and Castoria don't stare at me from hedges!" On seeing Queen Victoria, she wrote, ". . . a little, old, fat woman in black . . . a serene modest air . . . bowed slightly but graciously to the waiting and cheering crowds."

In another letter addressed to the entire family, she took special pains to reach her father, for Mr. Dennis had not been sympathetic to Ruthie's career and most certainly had resented the time, energy, and hovering protectiveness that his wife had showered upon this strange girl-child of his. It was in this atmosphere that

Ruthie wrote, "Go on building castles, Father dear. We have to build them first in thoughts always, only don't stop there. Try not to bite off more than you can chew, but having taken the bite chew it!"

At the end of the *Zaza* engagement in London, Ruthie made a brief excursion to Paris where she saw Loie Fuller, the American dancer, perform in her own theater, and where she came upon the lovely artifices of Japanese acting in a presentation by a Japanese actress. Both were to influence her career. Both Isadora and Miss Ruth were enormously impressed with La Loie, as the French called her. Isadora actually traveled with her and her company in 1902, although she did not perform with them, and it was Loie who presided over Isadora's Vienna debut. Isadora described Loie as this "luminous vision . . . I returned to the hotel dazzled and carried away by this marvelous artist."

Miss Ruth, many years later, referring to the origins of today's modern dance, felt that there had been a founding triumvirate at the turn of the century, Isadora, Loie, and herself. Certainly, Ruth St. Denis's lifelong concern with lighting effects may have been intensified by Loie's use of elaborate luminous devices to transform herself into a moth, a flame, a butterfly. She used complex props which she manipulated brilliantly, but her colors and suffusions of colors came from her own laboratory studies of lighting and phosphorescent materials. Ruthie Dennis was captivated.

She, in turn, captivated the men. There was something of the coquette about her, for she too had "roguish eyes," as did the great French ballerina of an earlier era, Madeleine Guimard. Those "roguish eyes" won for Guimard an impressive series of patrons, or "protectors," who showered her with jewels, money, even palaces. There were still "protectors" around when Ruthie came along and there were two, at this time, who would have welcomed a liaison with this fresh, talented young actress. One, of course, was Stanford White; the other, Belasco. In later years, St. Denis recalled that they were suave and expert in their patterns of seduction but that both were gentle and gentlemanly. When they discovered at the very start that Ruthie was not yet ready to accept a lover, a liaison, a "protector," they respected the stand of the virgin actress and deep friendships developed. White had long been a close friend, now he became a dearer one; and Belasco she came to love deeply as a daughter would a father.

Ruthie was by no means a prude. From earliest childhood, she responded to sensuous elements—the touch of her body against the grass, the caress of the sea, the warmth of the sun, the breezes that explored her body, even the rough work-hands of her iceman as he helped her alight from the buggy. But she was not yet, in London 1900, in need of sensual experiences. Romance, yes! Physical love, no! She would pose nude, as she did for her first professional photographer, James Breese, right after the Worth's Museum performances. But that was art. Stripping for social reasons was out. Ruthie was innocent but not naïve.

The career was all important, but she was not going

to forward it by a shrewd relationship, horizontal, with the boss. She was going to make it on her own. She and Mrs. Carter didn't like each other very much, but the great star spent little time thinking about a minor actress in her troupe. Ruthie could be impudent, and was, but she respected Mrs. Carter's art fully, even to the point of behaving like a fan. This odd combination of near impertinence and adoration on the part of the Jersey farm girl may have irritated the great actress, but it also made possible years of tours together.

Ruthie, who was to turn to acting from time to time throughout her long career as a world-famous dancer, learned a great deal from being with Mrs. Carter. She took note not only of her red hair, red nails, and her personal dressing room, which was transported wherever she traveled, but also of her use of gesture, movement, in her creation of roles. She also learned, perhaps to her initial surprise, that this Belasco favorite was a lonely woman, a state of being which was to cast its mark on Ruth St. Denis herself in the seventy years that still lay ahead of her.

The Belasco years continued. For Ruth St. Denis— Belasco had canonized her by this time, even if he had not been permitted to do anything else—the stage had become her home. Tours took place, but the places visited were soon dim. She was with Mrs. Carter in *Du-Barry*, in which she did a little dance but in which she also led the screaming mob as Du Barry was taken to the guillotine. The acting side was as important, as the dancing bit, perhaps more so. In an earlier Belasco play, *The*

Auctioneer, Ruthie through her antics had given two other girls the giggles. Belasco kept the trio as "the giggling girls" with a scene all their own.

It was discovered that Ruthie could also sing, and in *DuBarry* she sang "Amaryllis," a lovely air that was presumably composed during the reign of a happier Louis than Louis XVI, by the king himself, Louis XIII. This light, lyric, and sweet singing voice was to be used in later years on records and in conjunctions of dance and song in which she would be singer-dancer.

But Ruthie, energetic and irrepressible, the giggler and the "brain"—Belasco said that no one would capture her who did not capture her mind—kept herself from acute boredom on long tours by entertaining company and crew with jokes and acts in dialect, at which she excelled. She also relied upon the friendship of a fellow performer who was to play a part in the evolution of Ruth St. Denis, dancer. This was Honoria Donner, known as Nora, Patsy, or Pat. To St. Denis, she was "Pat."

Pat, with a quick Irish humor, joined with Ruthie in all kinds of pranks. Touring was a bore and the girls kept up each other's morale with backstage antics, gags, and just general companionship. Pat was also tuned in to her friend's shifting moods, to a restlessness that could not be explained away by boredom. Belasco was bewildered when Ruthie said that her dreams were as a dancer, not an actress. Pat Donner, whether she understood or accepted the fact, never questioned Ruthie's statement that her life must be with the dance.

Yet how could there be a future in dancing? She had given up the acrobatics of vaudeville for the art of Belasco. Ballet was dead. Genevieve Stebbins was but a childhood memory. It was not so much "why" a career as a dancer, but "how" and "where."

Athena, according to myth, sprang full grown from the head of Jove. Ruth St. Denis, whose art was to influence the entire world of dance and the theater, sprang from her own compulsions, mysterious, unanalyzable, but very real. Decades later, Jack Cole, dance choreographer for concerts, movies, television, and many Broadway musicals, noted that Ruth St. Denis, with no one to guide her, with no precedents in formulating a new dance, with nothing to copy, with hardly a clue, created a new world of dance . . . unaided. "When we use the word 'genius,' " he said, "now we know what we're talking about."

Deep inside, through the Belasco years and before, it was all there, but it needed a trigger or, creatively, a mating. It was the poster that did it. Only a poster advertising cigarettes, but from it came a new and glittering era in the theater.

CHAPTER IV

IT WAS just another tour day—or so it seemed. It was rainy and cold, and the tiny bedroom in the boarding-house was hideous. Ruthie got her best friend, her partner in pranks, her sounding board, Patsy Donner, to escape from their dreary surroundings and head for the drugstore for an ice-cream soda. This was routine, but also something of an adventure, and the ice-cream soda was to remain forever after the St. Denis weakness—not cigarettes, not liquor, but ice-cream sodas (along with oyster stew). On this occasion, whether the soda was especially good, standard, or disappointing has long since been forgotten, for after the first few sips, Ruthie's eyes strayed to the wall, to an advertisement, to THE POSTER.

The poster advertised Egyptian Deities, a brand of

cigarettes. The brand name was printed in large letters at the top; beneath it, as if it were an engraved inscription above the doorway of a temple, read the legend, "No Better Turkish Cigarette Can Be Made"; a reproduction of a box of the cigarettes was found at the bottom of the poster. It is what came in between that caused "a complete break in my life." The great in-between depicted a small temple, or niche, flanked by two columns bearing the lotus-crest capitals of ancient Egypt; there was also a pond of lotus blossoms; a wingéd scarab, holding a jewel, stretched across the top. In the aperture was a throne and on that throne sat a woman, serene, contemplative, regal, mysterious. It was Isis, modernized and commercialized, but it was the mother goddess of ancient Egypt.

Ruthie was hypnotized. In an instant, the past and the present fell away, and Ruth St. Denis had a creative experience which planted the seed which was to flower into one of the great careers in the theater. At first, she did not know that she had become pregnant with the art of dancing, but she knew something momentous had happened.

She had to have the poster. For some reason, she didn't trust herself to get it but sent a bewildered Patsy Donner to retrieve it from the drugstore even if she had to pay for it. She hung it on the wall at the foot of her bed and lost herself in it. All else fled her mind, and for the rest of the tour, which closed in San Francisco, she went through her chores in *DuBarry* simply by rote and occasionally cued by Pat. In every town, no matter how small, she rushed to libraries and museums to find whatever tidbit she could that would help her to create this work of her dreams, to bring this obsession to the theater. Thus was *Egypta* conceived. Until Ruthie got back home to her family, Patsy was her only confidante, the only one in the company to whom she dared explain that she had no intention of being an Egyptian dancer but that she intended to be Egypt herself, an entire nation as it lived the span of a day from dawn to dusk and from birth to death.

With the poster came a complete breaking with the past. There was no question about her continuing as an actress or a singer or as a show-business hoofer. She knew definitely that dance was to be her medium, but she also knew it was to be theater. The word "choreography" was unknown, and her concept of *Egypta* stemmed from ritual rather than from dance steps. This was unorthodox, unheard of at the turn of the century.

The form of *Egypta,* a full evening's dance drama, was perfectly clear to her. But where had it come from? The poster? The poster had triggered something that was already there inside this strange, talented, restless child. Looking back from the vantage point of 1960, Miss Ruth said in a talk we taped in her apartment, "What are the processes of creation in a person's mind, especially when something, apparently at right angles to what they had been doing, suddenly flowers? Without any argument, there it is in front of you, a tremendous inspiration.

"All I can say is that with my theory of the androgyne, in which every artist is both male and female, and that sometimes, the two great elements are in conjunction within him, so that all by himself he suddenly gets the melody and the burst of feeling of a great symphony without any external stimuli. At other times, a musician meets a woman, a painter sees the sunset, which are what I would call external stimuli, but the same conjunction takes place. In other words, he has to have that quality of soil which can be impregnated by the external. And this is what happened to me—the soil of Egypt must, unconsciously, have lain within me because my dance not only went to Egypt but it spread to the other countries of the Orient. In other words, without knowing it, I must have been half-Oriental."

The Poster was indeed the spark, the trigger, the catalyst that suddenly presided over the uniting of disparate elements, or seemingly so, of past experiences both within a lifetime, or, as Miss Ruth believed, in earlier lives. The Poster, as she said, "represented a complete break." Skirt dancing was unimportant, acting faded into the background, singing was a diversion. A whole new concept of theater possessed her. Swirling together were the art of Genevieve Stebbins, *The Burning of Rome, Egypt Through the Centuries,* flavored by readings from Dumas, Kant, and Eddy, plus a dimly remembered, but haunting, go at Mabel Collins's *The Idyll of the White Lotus.* Delsarte, of course, was there too. In the sense of the "divine androgyne," the Poster had impregnated her with a purpose that reached the channels of her own waiting fertility. Esthetically, it was something of a divine birth which was to come; in her eighties, with her sweet irreverence, she said, "If such a vision had happened within the church, I would have been a candidate for sainthood."

St. Denis hardly knew what happened during the remainder of the Belasco tour. When she got back from San Francisco, she gathered her family and tried to explain to them what had happened to her. There was no antagonism to her plan for a whole new world of theater; even Mr. Dennis supported his maverick daughter's incredible dream. Mother rallied, as always. Buzz was fascinated. With salt cellars, pepper shakers, and sugar bowls, Ruthie outlined *Egypta* on the dining-room table, and with all the gusto of a candidate for political office, she sold her family on *Egypta*. Pat Donner was already her secretary of state and general trouble-shooter, so project *Egypta* got under way. Ironically, however, it was not to be the work which launched the historic career.

Egypta, as she first conceived it, would have cost too much to produce, like three thousand dollars. Later, she was to earn that amount per week, but in 1903, no!

Her researches had led her to the Orient, not that of ancient Egypt, but the Orient of today. She knew little about it—certainly nothing firsthand—but from her encyclopedia readings, from trips to the Oriental strip at Coney Island, from her own inner visions, she began to make up simple Oriental dances that would cost nothing like *Egypta* would. But even these took money to costume and to rehearse; furthermore, it was necessary to keep the Dennis family going while the great transition was being planned and accomplished. She landed a job as a chorus singer in a show called *Woodland,* and this helped to pay the bills while she continued her researches and while she rehearsed her "scenes"—she thought of them as "scenes" rather than "dances" at this point—with a hodgepodge crew of Orientals she had assembled.

Rehearsals took place in the Dennis apartment—the family had moved to roomier quarters on Forty-second Street from the much smaller place on Fiftieth that had been home before the *DuBarry* tour. Ruthie not only rehearsed them in the street-scene that was to be the locale of her *Nautch* dance and, ultimately, *The Cobras,* but she also pumped them dry about East Indian lore, types of dress, customs, language, and even food! Japanese were also involved, and the whole soaking up procedure made her "a jolly jumble," as she described it later.

Her friendship with these Orientals proved helpful in many ways, for they could tell her where to go to buy materials and they introduced her to still others. So it was that she met an East Indian merchant whose shop was about to be visited by the fabulously rich Gaekwar of Baroda. The dance she gave was a preliminary sketch of *The Incense,* performed on a dais erected in the shop. Apparently the Gaekwar was pleased, and St. Denis, in her autobiography, recalls that the Rani complimented her by saying that she "looked and acted like a high-class Indian woman."

The Bhumgaras, who owned the shop, not only paid her for her performance but said she might have her

choice of any material in the store for a costume. Typical
of St. Denis, or, perhaps, any dedicated artist, she did not
pick the most expensive item in the shop. Her mind was
on her *Cobra* costume, and since the character was a
beggarwoman, the dress could not be rich. So she selected
a modest piece of brown material for a sort of wrap-
around covering and another nondescript piece for her
turban. The total cost was probably less than five dollars.
The costume lasted her throughout her long career, and
she used to swear, laughingly, that it had never been
washed! that keeping it dirty was pertinent to the filthy
beggar she was playing, and that it was so encrusted with
the years that it could stand alone!

In doing research for nautch dances, for street scenes
and temple dances, she came upon a theme perfectly
suited to her concept of theater. It was about the Hindu
Radha, beloved of the God Krishna, and in the story of
their love she found a dramatic, symbolic example of
man's search for contact with the divine. The need itself
she knew, and found her own personal pathway through
the Bible and the writings of Mary Baker Eddy; but here
was a way to present this need, this message, this vision
in theatrical terms. She thought of herself as a ritualist,
rather than a dancer, although the rhythms of dance
flowed through her, but within her dance dramas she
often included full-out dances where the theme demanded, in addition to acting and to ceremony.

In later years she mused about what would have happened if she had cast her quest for faith, for divine in-
volvement, in terms of Christian, instead of Hindu, ritual.

The chances are that she might never have been heard of. The Christian church, at that time, had no place for dancing in its services. Ritual was almost exclusively reserved for the Catholic mass, while most Protestant sects looked with suspicion on dancing of almost any kind. If she had explored the possibilities of a Christian dance liturgy at the turn of the century, she certainly would have had no theatrical outlet for her vast talent, and she would have been regarded as some kind of religious kook. As it was, her concept of a new theater, a new dance was beyond the comprehension of bookers, managers, and even audiences of the day, but the exotic trappings in which she cast religious tenets caught the fancy of the public. The shell was accepted, the content overlooked except by the very few.

But what of *Egypta?* It had first been set aside, temporarily, because of production expense, and the simple nautches were created in order to raise money for *Egypta,* but the truth of the matter was that St. Denis became fascinated with India (and Japan) and the plan for *Radha* became paramount in her mind. So it was that the historic debut program would not be Egyptian at all, but East Indian. Still the poster had started it all.

While the program was in the making, Ruthie earned money, as Isadora had, by dancing for social gatherings. She danced for Mrs. Stuyvesant Fish, the undisputed queen of New York's "400," and for other ladies of society. In excerpts from *Radha,* in the nautches, and in other Oriental bits, she was considered "charming" and "novel." She enjoyed what was then known as "a vogue."

This helped pay some of the bills but not all. The family —Mother, Buzz, Ruthie; Father was away—literally lived from day to day. There were no complaints, because they all believed in a dream.

Still, empty stomachs, "past due" notices, no funds for sets and costumes and fees for the Oriental associates made lucrative offers tempting. There was a Belasco tour offer, but it meant leaving everything behind, uncompleted. She was about to succumb to the stopgap job, when her beloved Countess Ada ("Aunt" Ada) ordered her to "stand firm" and gave her the last bit of cash she had. A society patroness, who recognized in her more than a "vogue," gave her two hundred dollars for the temple scene for *Radha*. A poor neighbor, a fellow churchgoer of Mother Dennis's, came over to the family kitchen and had Ruthie read the Bible in those passages which described, in some detail, the vicissitudes visited upon man, and then pinpointed the text which requires the believer to put his trust in the Lord. Ruthie cried, she believed, and she went ahead. For the rest of her long life, she put her faith in herself, and if that failed, in her God. As her husband once said, gently and with the patience of Job, "Sometimes she confuses the two."

Supplied with photographs and with Mother, Ruthie went from manager to manager, agent to agent, but no one wanted *Radha*. Undaunted, she rented a theater, empty at matinee time, and gave her new work, but the managers, all invited, never appeared and she performed for a charwoman. Finally, she went to the office of a well-known manager, Henry B. Harris. He took an interest in her and seemed impressed with her new theater. To show his faith, he paid for a matinee of *Radha* and invited his colleagues. They could hardly refuse him, so they turned out in force, a Hammerstein among them. But although each professed to be interested in the unusual newcomer, each felt her "act" was better for someone else.

From this showcase came an engagement in a New York theater for a Sunday night "smoking concert." The rough, tough men in the audience were pretty disenchanted when the curtain went up on an immobile Radha and a group of Hindu sailors wandering about as priests, but when Ruthie began to dance, they quieted down and at the close of the "Dance of the Senses," rewarded her with warm applause. She got a return date. A vaudeville engagement at Proctor's followed, where she was sandwiched between a boxer and a monkey act. The house program, in small print, gave the theme of *Radha,* including all the religious points, but then, in huge letters, it read, NOTE: THE ENTIRE DANCE WILL BE DONE IN BARE FEET.

Even in vaudeville, Ruthie attracted the attention of the discerning, so much so that a group of society ladies got together and sponsored a matinee at the Hudson Theater. Harris rented them the theater at a nominal fee and the historic program, all dance and including *The Incense, The Cobras,* and *Radha* (a seventeen-minute ballet). The date was March 22, 1906, almost two years after the Poster had changed the course of a life.

The twenty-five patronnesses, each paying twenty-five

dollars, were permitted to invite many guests, so the theater was filled. Incense was burning in the foyer and the ushers were dressed in a semblance of Oriental apparel—the Bhamgaras had been helpful in guiding Ruthie in her selection of costumes and fabrics and a young man, Edmund Russell, whom she had heard give a reading of *The Light of Asia,* became a valued friend and adviser. In vaudeville, Ruthie had been calling herself Radha, but now that she was to appear in other dances as well, a permanent, American name seemed in order. Mother suggested that she revert to her Belasco stage name, and so the career was to be that of Ruth St. Denis.

The matinee was a smashing success, so much so that Harris himself took over and continued to present a series of sold-out matinees at the Hudson. He remained her friend and manager until his death at the sinking of the *Titanic.*

The headlines in the New York papers literally screamed about the new sensation. They were baffled about her intent, but what they saw had them digging up every adjective they could find for "sensual." Yet underneath all the flap, they knew she was in no sense lascivious, depite displays of bare skin.

The advance newspaper publicity for the ladies' matinee included such choice bits as: "NO RUDE MEN MAY GAZE UPON THESE SENSUOUS DANCES." "MEN MUST PAY A WEEK LATER." "OF COURSE, SHE'S NOT ALL DRESSED, BUT IT'S ALL RIGHT TO THOSE WHO ARE ORIENTAL." This was printed in a bank of headlines. Earlier, before her "smok-

ing concert" appearance, the press had proclaimed: "NOT
A HINDOO, ONLY A JERSEY BUDDHIST. TOMORROW NIGHT SHE
WILL CAPER AS NIMBLY AT THE NEW YORK THEATER AS SHE
HAS AT MRS. STUYVESANT FISH'S." And again: "HER
COSTUME? AH, WELL, SHE WEARS A LITTLE JACKET, AND
A SKIRT OF GAUZE AND MAYBE AN ANKLET OR TWO."

In describing *Radha,* some of the reporters turned into
wiseacres, very probably because they were on uncertain
ground esthetically. One wrote, "She will be discovered
as a statue of the idol Radha, which lady by the way was
the favorite wife of Krishna, a gallant sort of person who
went about tooting on a conch and winning women's
hearts without number." The fact that Krishna did not
appear in the ballet, nor the Gopi maidens of myth, did
not stop this display of ethnic learning. One newspaper
settled for a simple headline: "FOUNDS NEW CULT."

Shortly after the Hudson Theater series had ended, St.
Denis was invited to dance in the palatial home of Boston's eccentric Mrs. Jack Gardner, who herself caused
Bostonians to gasp by wearing her pearls around her
waist instead of about her neck, walking about with a
wild animal on a leash, and crawling up the steps of her
church on her knees. With St. Denis, the proper Bostonians were dutifully shocked, far more than New
Yorkers. Their newspaper headlines included such gems
as: "BOSTON GASPS AS RUTH ST. DENIS DANCES" or "SOCIETY
REVIEWS ORIENTAL GYRATIONS IN FENWAY PALACE" or
"DARKNESS HID BLUSHES" or "BAREFOOT MAIDEN GIVES SO-
CIETY FOLK A NEW THRILL."

From Boston came an appraisal which would be

Above: Ruthie, Father, Buzz, Mother (about 1890). *Below left:* Ruth Dennis in the days down on the farm in New Jersey (about 1883). *Right:* Ruth Dennis, teen-age young lady. SIRI FISCHER-SCHEEVOIGHT

"The Giggly Girls" in a Belasco play–Ruthie is in the center (about 1900).

Ruth Dennis, the skirt dancer of vaudeville days (about 1895).
SCHLOSS, N.Y.

The famous cigarette poster which launched the great career. Seen in a drugstore in Buffalo, N.Y. during the transcontinental Belasco tour of "DuBarry."

The first costume (never actually used in performance) inspired by the poster. H. T. MOTOYOSHI, SAN FRANCISCO

"Radha"—the stage set, the company, and St. Denis in the Dance of the Sense of Sight (1906). WHITE, N.Y.

The Dance of the Sense of Touch from "Radha," which had Hugo von Hofmannsthal, the Viennese poet, in raptures. WHITE, N.Y.

Above: The Dance of the Delirium of the Senses, "Radha" (1906). To simulate the whirl of the skirt for the still camera, invisible threads were held by the photographer's assistants crouched out of camera range. *Below left:* Ruth St. Denis, taken in action, thirty-five years later, in the same backbend turn from "Radha" (1941). DWIGHT GODWIN. *Right:* "The Cobras." The emerald rings are the eyes of the two snakes. The arms are the snakes themselves. This dance was imitated throughout Europe and America.

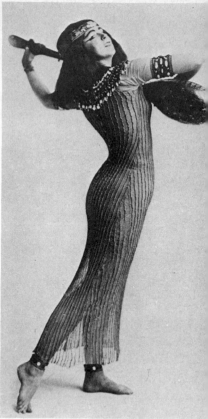

"Egypta," inspired by the cigarette poster, was finally produced in 1910. The settings were operatic in proportions. Note the "see-through" dress in certain scenes.

"The Incense" was the first dance in her East Indian repertory and opened the historic program at the Hudson Theater, New York, in 1906. Five years before her death at 91, she was still dancing it. This is an onstage candid taken in 1963. A year later, on the occasion of her Golden Wedding anniversary with Ted Shawn, she danced it at the Jacob's Pillow Dance Festival and subsequently on national television (CBS). She stood and moved for lighting designs, "blocked," rehearsed, and danced for approximately eight hours. She was 87 at the time.

"Bakawali," an East Indian ballet, and "O-mika," Japanese, both used dialogue as well as dancing (1913). *Above:* "Bakawali." *Below:* In "O-mika," St. Denis's Japanese speech was so perfect that Japanese in the audience translated it back into English without missing a word. Her samurai antagonist is, left, Brother St. Denis. PHOTOGRAPHS BY WHITE, N.Y.

In her first non-ethnic dance, "Scherzo Waltz." At a performance of this, she made news by defying a mayor and became "the mother of the strip tease." MOFFETT, CHICAGO

Ruthie and Mother at about the time she met Ted Shawn. New York, 1914. (Her hair had started to turn white when she was in her teens.)

Ruth St. Denis and Ted Shawn in one of their first duets after their marriage in 1914. NICKOLAS MURAY, N.Y.

"Ouled Nail," another duet. NICKOLAS MURAY, N.Y.

"Egyptian Ballet," performed thousands of times throughout the joint career of St. Denis and Shawn.

The famous Tillers of the Soil duet from "Egyptian Ballet." PUTNAM & VALENTINE, LOS ANGELES

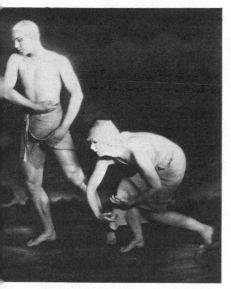

Right: A revival of The Tillers duet at Jacob's Pillow forty years later. JOHN LINDQUIST, BOSTON

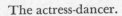
The actress-dancer.

"Miriam, Sister of Moses" (1919).
MACGREGOR

Nudity, or near-nudity, was revealed as purity by St. Denis (right) and girls at Denishawn, Los Angeles. *Below:* On tour with Denishawn. B. ST. DENIS

Above: St. Denis visits her soldier-husband. HAROLD TAYLOR, CORONADO, CAL. 1918. *Below left:* St. Denis and Shawn in a Spanish dance. She was better at shawls and skirts than with heel-beats. "Teddy was the Spanish dancer in the family." *Right:* St. Denis, the star. NICKOLAS MURAY, N.Y.

typical of the reaction Ruth St. Denis would draw in America—not in more sophisticated Europe—for a good many years to come. It said, in part, " 'Cold Roast' Boston sat up and took notice for about an hour yesterday in Fenway Court and rubbed its eyes at the spectacle of a barelegged maiden who put the Persian dancers on the Midway in the shade. Two hundred fifty representative men and women paid five dollars for 'sweet charity's sake' to see her gyrations and contortions, and then they gasped. . . . Ruth St. Denis was born on a New Jersey farm which is a long way from Bombay and Calcutta. Nevertheless, she has hit the taste for novelties, and there you are! Her stunts are sensational from any point of view, and yet none of her dances are open to the charges of vulgarity."

Caroline and Charles Caffin in their *Dancing and Dancers Today,* published by Dodd, Mead in 1912, perceived and reported on the American public's response to this new genius, sensuous, yet pure. Of the Proctor engagement they wrote, "The vaudeville audience as a whole did not comprehend her aspirations. At first, there was a distinct gasp of amazement, wonderment whether to disapprove of the audacity or to resent the lofty conception." The theatergoers of 1906 could not reconcile the two, the relating of beauty of body with beauty of spirit.

The Caffins made careful note, as did the vaudeville managers of the day, that Ruth St. Denis was attracting new audiences, people who came again and again to see *Radha* and who left the minute it was over. For the

harried reporters and for the average theatergoer, there
was no precedent by which to judge the new star. Exposed skin and body undulations should mean carnival
side shows, honky-tonks, sex; somehow, with Ruth St.
Denis they did not. Pagan theories, a philosophy about
the renunciation of physical desires should be for the
professors, for the dilettantes, for the nuts on the fringe
of society; but Ruth St. Denis made them theater. No
wonder audiences were bewildered. No wonder reporters
contradicted themselves only sentences apart by compar-
ing her with midway dancers and then adding, rather in
surprise, that she wasn't vulgar. One reporter, in the
South a few years later, described her physical charms in
some detail and then concluded, perhaps against his
better judgment, that "there is something surprisingly
spiritual about her."

For us today, familiar with dances as part of church
services, dance works which are deeply rooted in the
aspirations of man, serious plays and films in which
total nudity prevails, the reaction to Ruth St. Denis, her
body, and her spirit in 1906 seems childlike if not
childish. But the art of dancing, in America, was at its
lowest ebb. It was trivial and it was supposed to be trivial.
Ruth St. Denis made the stage her altar; the theater, her
church. That she was intensely theatrical simply assured
her success; that she was utterly sincere in her determination to restore to dance in America what India, Japan,
China, and most of the rest of the world expected of
dance—that the dancing body represented life on a
higher plane—was inarguable. The press and public, in

America of 1906, sensed this but didn't understand it, didn't relate to it. But they loved the show.

The show they saw was *The Incense, The Cobra* (frequently it was billed in the plural as *The Cobras*), and *Radha*. And just what did they see?

THE INCENSE. The stage is draped with gray curtains; two stands from which incense arises are placed downstage right and left. The light is dim, for this is purdah, the carefully screened women's quarters, and it is about dawn. The back curtains part, and a high-caste Hindu woman, dressed in a gray sari, enters bearing a tray from which wisps of smoke rise. Alone, away from the temple, she is praying to the gods at the start of a new day. She moves slowly, quietly. She approaches one stand and crumbles some incense upon the embers, and as the curl of smoke coils upward, one of her arms mirrors this action in the subtlest of ripples. With gentle tread, she moves to the second stand and repeats the ritual. Then, at center stage, she places her incense tray on the ground, and as the smoke rises, her arms begin to ripple as if they were without joint or bone. The ripple appears to begin in the shoulders, then, wavelike, courses down the arms, through the fingers and out into space. The body, ever so subtly, echoes this ripple in just a hint of sinuosity in the torso. At one moment, she stands utterly still except that the hand bearing the tray moves slowly upward, almost hugging the body and head, until the dancer herself seems to have become a holy stele, a column of truth, or, perhaps, a stilled human receptacle for divine illumination. At the close, the gray-clad worshipper retreats to the gray curtains, which seem to envelop her, conceal her. She is gone.

THE COBRAS. It is a street in India. The sun falls yellow and hot on a bazaar where women and merchants are haggling, beggars are pleading, jugglers are entertaining, and a yogi walks in deep thought. Two street musicians, a drummer and a flutist, enter along with a dirty, evil-looking woman with arms crossed and hands, unseen, hanging over her shoulders. She wears a dirty, rusty dress and a turban from which wisps and straggles of black hair appear. The musicians set up a platform for her. Bored, she settles herself on it and the music begins. Now her sleeved arms disentwine themselves from her neck, and the hands come into view. On the index and little fingers of each hand, she is wearing huge emerald rings. They glare as if they were eyes, and indeed they are, the eyes of a pair of cobras. The eyes look balefully at the passers-by, the seemingly hooded heads (the hands are contracted at the knuckles) weave back and forth on the long stems of the arms as if they would strike. They slither over and around the head of the snake charmer; they poise; they are on the alert; they shock; they hypnotize. Then, at the moment of climax, the two heads come together and strike a double death! The scene ends, purposely, on a note of evil anticlimax. The snake charmer, having risen from her platform for the strike at the audience, now turns away to leave the bazaar. With a toss of a shoulder, one snake arm crosses her body

and comes to rest on the other shoulder; the other repeats the pattern and the woman leaves with the snake
heads hanging down her back and the emerald eyes
watching the audience.

RADHA. The scene is a temple. A light falls on the
immobile, bronze figure of Radha. It is dim and blue,
and the figure takes on a mystic, half-real, half-dream
semblance of life. Priests are present. They move through
ancient rituals as they seek guidance from the figure of
the goddess. Suddenly, a miracle occurs. Their faith rewards them, for the eyelids of the statue move, then a
breath causes the bronze bosom to move, and the statue
comes alive and steps down from the dais to teach, in
dance, the pathway to heaven, to nirvana. The five senses
are the key. Sight is satisfied by the luster or pearls, the
jewels which bedeck her body, and she devours their
luminosities. Hearing is caressed by the tinkle of bells
which she wears on her fingers, and she leans into the
beauty of sound. She selects garlands of flowers and
presses them against the contours of her body, inhaling,
absorbing heady fragrances as she favors the sense of
smell. With touch, she strokes her own body, feels the
loveliness of her limbs, lies on the floor, prone, and
slowly brings her fingers up to her lips. With the sense
of taste, she raises a bowl to her lips and drinks. The
heady wine arouses her, and she almost reels in ecstasy.
And then the total desires of the senses take over, and in
a wildly sensual climax, the goddess, dressed in gold and
with a great golden skirt swirling about her, gives herself

up to the "Delirium of the Senses" in a dizzying dance spinning ecstasy. Spent, she falls to the floor. Next she discards the golden skirt of earthly value, and returns to the dais where she assumes again the posture of serenity and chastity. She has delivered, perhaps in fact, perchance in vision, her message of the Renunciation of the Senses. This is her sermon, told in exotic terms but none the less profound.

It is easy to see how reporters and audiences of 1906 latched onto the delirium of the senses and gave short shrift to the message of renunciation. After all, dance was supposed to be trivial; if you wanted a sermon you went to church. What few understood was that the theater was Ruth St. Denis's church. As far back as 1906, she pondered on the suitability of the theater as a home for her rituals. But where could she go? The church was not ready for her, and fortunately for the history of dance, only the theater could give her a showing.

And to this theater she contributed not only a new dance and a new concept of stylized drama, but also an array of production devices we now take for granted. She wanted lights—her concern with lights very probably came from her brief exposure to the art of Loie Fuller—to change during a given scene. This was unheard of. Colored gels were changed *between* scenes, not in performance. But Ruthie insisted. Brother Buzz was her lighting expert, stage manager, and even co-dancer. Together they worked out a plan, mainly Brother's, whereby a light could be lowered or raised in a cylinder which had multicolored "windows." Thus, ambers and pinks and blues could be quickly shifted. From this primitive device, it is thought that the "pinwheel" color device, used today, evolved.

Brother, with his father's inventiveness, definitely worked out the then miraculous lighting effect which had Radha suffused in light, at the start and at the conclusion of her dance, from above. In 1968 Brother St. Denis, in his eighties, told me, "I invented a cage moved by ropes across the top of the theater. I sat in it and directed an overhead light on Ruth as Radha. She was always nervous about the lighting at the close, but I focused the lights on her—we called them klieg lights in those days—and I was always there, directly over her throne, to put the light on her. I've been stuck up there, but I don't think we ever missed the light cue in America, in Europe, in the Orient."

After the five Belasco years—1899–1904—there had been two years of preparation, years of incredible hardship and near hunger and despair; but the strength of Mother Dennis, the concern of Kate Dalliba, who put up two hundred dollars for the *Radha* set and gave her faith with it, the Countess Ada, who gave her last twenty dollars toward the new career, Mrs. Orlando Rouland (wife of a painter), who organized the famous Hudson matinee, and a Mrs. Barrett, who went to church with Mrs. Dennis and who got out the Bible and had Ruthie read from it when all seemed hopeless, all played their distinctive parts in launching a career that not one of them dreamed, except maybe Ruthie, would spread its influence around the world.

Deeply concerned with the religious nature of her mission, St. Denis accepted whatever housing, secular or sanctified, was offered to her. Her irrepressible wit did not reject the fun that the stagehands of 1906 poked at her sacred dances, for she herself used to say that as she came into the theater, the crew would yell, "Here she is boys, now lets get the goddess lit!"

Brother St. Denis, in 1968, spoke of her dedication, her concern with religion, but then gave his practical appraisal of the sister he "lit," beginning in 1906: "She always had a tremendous drive for dance, but I remember most her love for show business. She was interested in many things, but show business was first."

CHAPTER V

AFTER the sensational debut in New York as an artist (she had already been on the boards as a hoofer-actress for a decade and more) and the dazzling success in Boston, Europe came next. Harris had booked her for a series of matinees at the Aldwych Theater in London. In addition, she had introductions to society figures, and as in New York, these proved important both from the prestige point of view and for financial reasons (New York and Boston successes had not brought in much money).

Ruthie, Mother, and Pat Donner arrived in London—Father and Buzz came later—on May 31, 1906. Her first performance was for the Duchess of Manchester, and there were later performances for the Earl of Lonsdale and other members of high society. Among those who saw her and admired her were King Edward VII, who offered personal congratulations to her; United States Ambassador and Mrs. Whitelaw Reid; and of arts notables, John Sargent and Loie Fuller. Then came the first matinee, July 5, at the Aldwych. "Went very well," she wrote in her journals, but the "receipts were only eight pounds." (Three years later she would be back in London, not for three matinees, but for ten weeks, as a solo performer at the Coliseum, for five hundred pounds a week.)

The next day she did a charity affair for "a charming audience," and on July 9, the Earl of Lonsdale provided her with "a small stage, very pretty" and a "cold" audience. The second matinee, July 10, attracted "a small but enthusiastic audience . . . the Maharaja of Kapurthala came around to my dressing room and congratulated me. Receipts, fifty-eight pounds. . . . I went out and bought a beautiful black wig for street wear." (St. Denis, now nearing thirty, had long had a great deal of white hair mixed with the brown.)

On the twelfth, she gave her closing matinee. Mrs. Patrick Campbell, the great actress, came backstage to compliment her warmly, and there were booking agents from the Continent. One of these was the manager of the Folies Bergère, another was a Mr. Marinelli, who offered her an engagement at the famous Olympia in Paris for three hundred dollars a week. She refused the offer and was literally threatened with a statement that he controlled all the variety houses in Paris and that she could not get in without him. Another agent, a fair-haired

Russian named Braffe, offered her an engagement at the one theater not under the direct influence of the impresario who had subjected her to dire threats. The theater was the Marigny, and "Braffie," as she was soon to call him, booked her for an engagement, herself and her company of Hindus and stringers and, as she once said, "probably ne'er-do-wells among 'em."

There was to be a lull before the Paris debut, so Braffe arranged for Ruthie, the Dennis family, and the troupe to have a French vacation. She had insufficient funds, but he raised the money for the young dancer he believed in and in whom he had a romantic interest. On July 28 Ruthie and Braffe left the vacation retreat to journey quickly to Paris, where they "went to the Marigny Theater, the place where I am to dance. God help me, and I know he will. Divine love has met, and always will meet, every human need."

But the worst was to come. In early August, before the Marigny season, the Olympia Theater, controlled by the agent whom she had turned down, announced the first appearance of "Madame Radha, the Original Hindu Temple Dancer." She was, of course, an imposter. Ruthie went to see her and was dismayed by the crass imitation. Press and public were disenchanted, but that did not help. The Marigny management got cold feet and did everything it could to break its contract with Ruth St. Denis. With recourse to the law, she held to her rights and the Marigny debut was assured. But other obstacles were placed in her way. In her journals she wrote, "The manager of the Marigny says I cannot use the *Lakmé* music but that the leader of the orchestra can arrange new music . . . for two hundred dollars (racket?)." In 1968 Brother St. Denis said, "I'll *never* forgive the French for the way they treated us."

On August 22 everything was at an impasse. "I should not be surprised," wrote Ruthie, "if we never played the Marigny at all. Still, if we do, then God must open the door."

Behind the scenes, Braffe was at work: the Marigny honored the contract; the new orchestration was made; and a movielike publicity stunt had Ruth St. Denis the daughter of an Indian aristocrat and a French officer!

Finally, the time arrived. August 31. "Tonight was the press performance—success!" On September 1 was the formal debut, and Ruth St. Denis became the toast of Paris. The fake Radha was forgotten and the real artist was acclaimed. In the report of her debut, the stunned dancer made one of her rare understatements: "Everybody satisfied." Then added, "Artists came to sketch me." Among them was Rodin.

The season was a triumph. There were "mobs outside waiting to see me." The Baron and Baronness de Rothschild not only came to the dressing room to congratulate her but also invited her to visit their home. Europeans and fellow Americans showered her with praise and adulation. The French press and the American press recorded her success; her art was seriously discussed in articles, essays, and interviews. Poems and poems in prose celebrated her; one was by the famous American poetess, Ella Wheeler Wilcox (1850–1919), who wrote, *"Radha* is a dance and a hymn, a prayer, a picture, and an epic poem all in one. Here is another woman who has created a new thing in art, and again in the realm of Terpsichore. Let her name go into the Hall of Fame. She has elevated her art and given the world a beautiful work." Mrs. Wilcox's reference to her as "another woman" in the world of dance indicates that she had seen Isadora Duncan a few seasons before in Paris or, perhaps, both Isadora and Loie Fuller.

On October 10 Ruthie, unaccompanied by Mother, visited Rodin's studio to have him sketch her arms. She removed her shirtwaist in order for him to observe the shoulder and arm ripples, which he sketched; he also attempted to make love to her with words of praise and passion, and with kisses. She escaped, for although she was a woman and no longer a girl, the need for physical love had not yet awakened in her—romance, even courtship, yes, but activated physical love, no. The French, indeed, were surprised that such a beautiful, voluptuous woman did not have a "protector," and they were almost disbelieving when it was made clear that the only protection Ruth St. Denis required at this moment in her life was provided by Mother and by her constant chum and companion, Brother Buzz.

Spiritual love, however, was a necessity. She discussed matters of the spirit with Mother; she found constant haven in the writings of Mrs. Eddy; and before going on stage, she would devote time to contemplation, to purifying her being for the temple dances to follow. She needed some such comfort, for although she was familiar with vaudeville houses, smoking concerts, and even a monster museum, she had never before faced up with anything like a French variety house, which she found dismal and dirty and where the stagehands were sloppy and drunk. Still, she stuck it out, playing to capacity houses not only for the four scheduled weeks of her engagement but also for an unprecedented holdover of two more weeks.

The Paris smash hit of Ruth St. Denis echoed across Europe, and Braffe had no trouble booking her for a winter tour. The first stop was the Komische Oper in Berlin.

Her first appearance was in the Street Scene in the Délibes opera *Lakmé,* but soon afterward she commenced dancing her own programs. From the start, Berlin took her to its heart. In her journals, she wrote, "They really rose to me and cried Bravo, Bravo! again and again. It was fine!" Her attire, however, came under official scrutiny, for although she was treated politely by the police, she was asked to submit to investigation. In *Lakmé,* she had been seen only as the well-covered snake charmer in *The Cobras,* but at the triumphant press preview she had done *Radha* with bare legs and midriff. The police were alerted and Braffe brought the investigating squad to check for themselves. The outcome, Ruthie describes in her journals: "Well, the morals of the German public are preserved! The government, preceded by Braffie, came to inspect my waistline! I turned and twisted evidently to their satisfaction, since I may continue to paint my tummy!"

There were a few reviews of the smart-alecky school,

but for the most part, Ruth St. Denis was accorded a press response which combined deep admiration with profound respect, analysis of her new art with the poetry of discovery. For the two years that she danced, almost without rest, in Germany, Austria, Hungary, she would be welcomed as an equal into exclusive circles of artists, intelligentsia, society. In fact, one of the very first reviews of her was written by the great Viennese poet, Hugo von Hofmannsthal (creator of many librettos, among them *Elektra,* for Richard Strauss), who called her "The Incomparable Dancer" and wrote: "In this extraordinarily hieratic art—strange combination of a strangely alive being with primeval tradition—every trace of sentimentality has vanished. It is the same with her smile, and so it is that from the first moment, she estranges the hearts of women and the sensual curiosity of men on seeing Ruth St. Denis. And it is just this that makes her dancing incomparable. It borders on voluptuousness but it is chaste. It is consecrated to the senses, but it is a symbol of something higher. It is wild, but bound by external laws. It could not be other than it is. I saw her for a quarter of an hour, and there were moments—such as falling down, kissing her own fingers, drinking from the bowl—that have impressed themselves upon the memory as does a noble detail from the Elgin marbles or a color of Giorgione. She will take her own place wherever she appears. Her wonderful directness— that severe almost repellant directness—her sublime earnestness which is without a touch of pedantry, all this creates about her that isolation that ever surrounds the extraordinary."

Although Germany treated her as a goddess, as a creative artist of unparalleled importance, she herself found it difficult to respond easily, much less, enthusiastically, to Germanic art expressions of the time. She recognized the vigor of Strauss and came to respect his art, but music of a lyrical nature, melodic, was always more to her liking. She would have preferred the earlier Strausses, the Johanns, to Richard. Nevertheless, she was a frequent participant in gatherings attended by the playright Wedekind, and such other leading figures in the world of culture as Hauptmann, Richter, and Count Kessler. With von Hofmannsthal, however, she had a close relationship. It was by no means a love affair, but it was an affair of the minds and of the spirit. Her interest wandered from these groups because *Egypta* was once again stirring within her, and she knew that in Berlin she would be able to study in one of the great centers of Egyptology, not only observing fabulous collections of ancient art but also talking with, asking, probing, learning from, German Egyptologists.

Wherever she went in Germany and Austria, both the general public and the intellectuals and arts colonies hailed her. She reports that for the first time in Europe she was not treated as an entertainer but as an artist; and Brother St. Denis, who served as her business manager as well as her stage manager and lighting expert, speaking of his sister in 1969, more than sixty years after her Berlin debut, said very simply, "The Germans were crazy

about her. They gave her a wonderful reception everywhere. The French treated her abominably behind the
scenes; they cheated her. Not Germany. I remember that
we played the Hansa Theater, a vaudeville house, in
Hamburg. Ruth and the rest of us performed for a
month, but we stayed one extra day and got paid in gold
coins!" Brother also remembers that imitators, even pre-
tenders, were to be found here. Paris had its Madame
Radha, who quickly disappeared, and Germany had a
Ruth St. Donis, who faded fast. But in the variety houses
of Europe and very quickly in America, the real St.
Denis would be imitated in her temple dances, and
especially in such pieces as *The Cobras*.

From the Oper in Berlin, St. Denis went to one of
Europe's most renowned variety theaters, the Winter-
garten. There she played for close to two months, reaching an audience that was younger, less sophisticated, but
vital and curious. Her immense popularity brought its
problems. Finances were in good order. Mother and
Brother St. Denis were constantly present as buffers,
organizers, managers, and the "protectors" that made a
"lover-protector" unnecessary. Every manager wanted
her, so there was the inevitable law suit claiming, "She
promised to come here," "She said she would do this,"
etc. She won such suits easily, because she was eminently
fair in all her dealings, but she was disturbed by them.

She was even more disturbed by thoughts and feelings
which went on within herself. She adored the opportunity in Berlin to do research on Egyptian and Oriental
backgrounds; she adored being received as an artist

rather than as an entertainer; she adored it when crowds outside the theaters cheered her and even blocked her way to her carriage; and she adored being adored. But was she doing what the Poster had set her out to do on one of the strangest quests in the history of the theater? Was she just a dancer, exotic and admired, or was she getting across a spiritual message rooted in her own conscience and colored almost equally by the Lord Shiva and Mary Baker Eddy.

The performances continued to be rousing successes, no matter how she felt inside. The workload was enormous, for sometimes, at the Oper, dance appearances were sandwiched in matinees between operas, and although Berlin was to remain her headquarters, she toured to Dresden, Dusseldorf, Hamburg, and other German cities. Somehow, during this period, she found time to work on two new dances. One was *Nautch,* which she had originally sketched when she first began her experimenting with *Radha,* and then dropped as the temple scene took shape. The second was *The Yogi.* Both had their world premières in Vienna, and both were to remain in her active repertory for sixty years!

Nautch, of course, was a secular dance. The nautch girl might perform at a bazaar, outside a temple, or in the palace of a maharajah. Ultimately, St. Denis created a number of nautch dances, and they became the rage of the Western theater world, for it was she who introduced the nautches to the Occidental theater with such success that not only were they imitated by professionals but they would soon become essential to the training of ambitious dance students, for they would serve as routines and, their movement elements broken down and codified, as a new technical approach to dance instruction. This, however, would not be developed on a large scale until the founding of the nation-wide, in America, Denishawn schools by St. Denis and Shawn.

This first *Nautch,* often designated as "The Green Nautch" because of the predominant color in the costume, was later recostumed in dazzling white and was then referred to as "The White Nautch." But it was the same dance. A later solo, *Dance of the Black and Gold Sari,* which all of India would cheer twenty years in the future, was sometimes called *Dance of the Red and Gold Sari,* if St. Denis elected to change saris. *The Yogi* also underwent costume changes. When first done in Vienna, the dancer wore a black wig of comparatively straight hair, a sort of vest which left the middle bare, and an above-the-knees wrap closely resembling the traditional Indian dhoti. In later years St. Denis wore a filmy garment of pink, with a jagged hemline close to the ankles, and she combed her own white hair into a marvelous wind-swept effect.

These two new dances represented for the young dancer important choreographic advances, although she had never heard of the word "choreography" at that time. *Nautch,* with its yards and yards of material in the skirt, culminated in fast turns which had the drapes billowing out into space. The dancer also manipulated the materials, making them froth and foam or swirl around her arms. In the "Delirium of the Senses" dance from

Radha, the culminating turns were of the nautch variety, but here, in the new solo, the slick, skillful entertainer, rather than the goddess, was depicted. In addition to the climactic spins there was a spicy walk in which the dancer, moving in profile to the audience, dragged first one foot then the other as she made the ankle bells trill out a message of loveliness. And as she moved, she held her body in a very slight backbend, the shoulders back and the pelvis forward as hands and arms reached out into space caressingly, provocatively. Of subsequent nautches, all popular, the only one that matched the original ("green" or "white") in popularity was the one for which the American composer, Charles Wakefield Cadman, wrote the music on commission. This was the nautch in which the street dancer asked for *baksheesh!* (money) and not getting it, cursed the passers-by. Much later, these two nautches became to dance, in a miniature way, what the operas *I Pagliacci* and *Cavalleria Rusticana* are in everyone's mind—you can't imagine one without the other.

The Yogi was totally different. The devout, undiverted servant of god strides onto the scene. Across the back is slung a musical instrument. The step is inexorable, the eyes look neither to right nor left. This is a mission, a quest. The leg sweeps high, an arm makes a spiral gesture, and the hand rushes upward as if it would probe heaven itself. Then comes a moment of pause, and the yogi sits cross-legged on the ground in repose. This is a lesson in contemplation, in meditation. The arms and hands move in gestures of search, supplication, and prayer. In intense quietude, the yogi achieves a state of bliss and, rising, marches off to the far horizons of the spirit.

This was a daring dance to do in 1908, and perhaps only Austria or Germany would have given it immediate homage. For here was a dance that was actually focused on *inaction,* a ritual in which the action was of an inner nature. Through concentration, through a felt dynamic strength, St. Denis held the attention of her audience. "Through her mere 'being there,' " wrote a Viennese critic, "Ruth St. Denis facinates her audience." St. Denis herself, by this time, had studied yoga and was impressed with its relating of the disciplines of the body with the discipline of the mind. She herself practiced yoga exercises (including standing on her head daily) and meditation for the rest of her life.

The first production of *Nautch,* which was the first of her dances to use authentic East Indian music (performed by an Indian musician), was set in an elaborate palace scene. Many years later, in concert, she often performed it as a solo on an unadorned stage. *The Yogi* at first was done in a forest setting with a shaft of sunlight coming through the trees. The music was composed by her favorite European conductor, Walter Meyrowitz, and at the Vienna première had a prelude in which the audience could hear the singing of yogi pilgrims.

These two dances were very frequently added to *The Incense, The Cobras,* and *Radha* and presented under an overall title, *The Five East Indian Dances.* Hermann von Kaulbach, one of Germany's great painters, painted her in *Nautch*—this was later on view at the Metropolitan Museum of Art in New York—and in *The Incense*.

From 1906 to late 1909, when she returned to America, Ruth St. Denis's European engagements not only included Berlin and a host of German cities, but also Vienna, Budapest, Brussels, Monte Carlo, London (on several occasions), and other cities in the United Kingdom. Brother was with her all the time; Mother, most of the time. There is a "Miss Ruth" story, part-true and part-apochryphal, which has to do with Mother's organized methods as distinct from Ruthie's instinctive, mercurial behavior. St. Denis not only changed costumes and settings for her dances, as whim or circumstance dictated, but she was also given to changing the dances themselves. When she was alone on stage, or doing a solo while the rest of the cast was not choreographically involved with her, this air of improvisation worked, for she was a supreme dancer, and like Isadora, an instinctive one. The story goes that while working on *Nautch* in Vienna, she kept changing the choreography in rehearsals until the cast was on the brink of a nervous breakdown. Her reason for the changes was simply that she got bored with what was being rehearsed and kept inventing new movements and patterns.

Mother, who had been away, was either sent for or arrived in the nick of time, and as she walked into a rehearsal said, "Ruthie, whatever you have just done now stays, good or bad. No more changes." The legend continues that Ruthie threw herself on the floor, screamed, and wept. But to no avail. Mother was adamant. The cast sighed, and the show went on.

All through her long career, St. Denis was given to improvising. One of her dancers once said, "I think Miss Ruth has key places in all of her dances and she always gets to them on time, but what she does in between varies from performance to performance." Shawn tells some hilarious stories of how he would direct her, *sotto voce*, in performance on where to go to next! Left to her own devices, she was unfailingly effective, but it was sometimes difficult for her to adjust her own inspirational movements to the routines of others. In Vienna the pattern began, but Mother saved the day.

Her success swelled across Europe and she was in demand everywhere. She hated Budapest—"a terribly depressing city"—but Vienna and the German towns were much more to her liking. The German art of the day, while intensely vital and vigorous, she found a little too harsh for her taste. As an old lady, she would often use foreign phrases, a few in German but the majority in French, for although she had nowhere the success in France that she had in Germany, French culture appealed to her, as it did to Isadora.

London, of course, made amends for its initial small-scale interest in her, and she returned to play a season at the La Scala Theater and engagements at the Coliseum which netted her five hundred pounds a week. Late in 1909 she set sail for home. She could have stayed. If she had agreed to remain in Germany for two more years, a Ruth St. Denis Theater would have been built, but the longing for her homeland was too great, and in triumph she returned to America for unprecedented dance successes on Broadway and on tour.

The next phase of the career had begun.

CHAPTER VI

With Europe's stamp of approval on her, St. Denis returned home with the assurance that she was now, in the minds of her countrymen, a major American star, albeit a dancer and a maverick. In November, under Harris's management, she returned to the Hudson Theater for a series of sold-out matinees. The next month she gave a week of evening performances, also sellouts, which represented the first time in American history that a solo dancer had played an evening series on Broadway. A combination of matinees and evenings followed at the Hudson and then an enormously successful tour of the eastern part of the country, with extensive engagements in Chicago and Boston and performances in such major cities as Baltimore, Cincinnati, Philadelphia, Pittsburgh, Rochester, St. Louis, and lastly, in the spring of 1910, back to the city where it all started with the Poster, Buffalo.

During this tour, the sixth of the East Indian dances was added to the series, *The Lotus Pond,* with a score by Meyrowitz. Since St. Denis always thought, creatively, in terms of "scenes," it is interesting that in subtitles for each of the six, she indicated locales; thus, she represented Purdah (*Incense*), The Street (*Cobras*), The Temple (*Radha*), The Palace (*Nautch*), The Forest (*Yogi*), and The Garden (*The Lotus Pond*).

In Europe, she had listed these dances as East Indian, for Europeans had no reason to confuse the peoples intended with the Indians of America, East or West, whom they thought of as red men. In America the reverse was true, and it is likely that for this reason St. Denis, on her first major United States tour, listed her bill as "A Program of Hindoo Dances."

Commenting in her journals about her return to America in 1909, she made her key statements succinctly: "Back in New York after three years." "Big success." As the years went by, entries in the journals became more regular, more soul-searching, and of much greater length —a sort of secret confessional.

With her return home in 1909 and with the European honors clearly recorded, vulgar humor by helplessly unprepared reporters became a thing of the past. There were, of course, no dance critics in those days, simply because dance, before the coming of Duncan and St. Denis, had been of no moment for more than half a century. But now that St. Denis had made her mark with royalty, with von Hofmannsthal, with Rodin, with the important minds of Europe, America was alerted. In Boston, she received the attention of one of the nation's great music critics, Philip Hale. He wrote about her in his fine, colorful prose, and while paying just tribute to her art, he almost made love to her in print as he did to no musical personality:

"In comparison with the dancing of Ruth St. Denis, the posturing, the prancing, the loping, the bounding of Isadora Duncan seem common and material. It is true that Miss St. Denis has advantages over the majority of her sisters in art. She is tall and of entrancing proportions. From the sole of her foot to the crown of her head she is apparently without blemish. Her knees might well have moved the Singer of Solomon's Song to rapture. The ensemble of her body is as a flawless lyric.

"And yet there is this to be said that to some might be paradoxical: although her body is that of a woman divinely planned, there is no atmosphere of sex about her whether she is immovable upon the altar—a picture of beauty never to be forgotten—or dancing the sense of touch." And this from one famed for his erudite annotations of the great symphonies!

1910. At last, it was possible to do *Egypta,* with Harris as the producer. Elaborate sets, a large cast, lavish contumes, unprecedented scenic and lighting effects, and a special score by Meyrowitz were now possible. Six years after exposure to the Poster, here was its fruit. In an exclusive, taped interview with me in the quiet of a New York studio, she described the historic *Egypta* as she had created it. More than fifty years had passed, but its impact remained in her own mind—she was past eighty—a recollection of blazingly clear theatrical images, adjudicated by her own irrepressible and irreverent wit. I reproduce her words verbatim, for they exist nowhere in the world except on recording tape made especially, at my insistence, for me, whom she referred to, in passing, as "my historian."

Egypta, then, as told by Ruth St. Denis herself; how she conceived it, how she choreographed it, how it was staged:

"The intellect is the servant of the spirit, isn't it? The intellect of itself is not a very valuable thing. When it sets up on its own it isn't. When it is obedient, it is wonderful. I think whatever budding intellect I had, whatever surface intelligence, shall we say, was set to work on the task of how *would* I dance Egypt. It finally evolved, without going into it in a too involved way, into the life of Egypt in one day and one night, as being symbolic of the life of Egypt . . . see, I started being symbolic and I've kept quite steadily at it ever since! . . . but this was my first with symbolism, and it was that she, Egypt, did certain things from morning to midnoon, to noon, to midafternoon, and then she was defeated and began to die, and she died on the steps of the throne on which she had sat. This means she had completed the cycle of the day of twelve hours. Well, to fill in what the Egyptians did took some 'readin'.' And I haunted with dear Pat Donner, who had thought that I'd gone quite cuckoo, the museums, because I wanted to know what the priests wore, what the fellahin did, and when did the kingship arrive at its apotheosis, and when was the Persian Conquest and all those things, which were information, they weren't even culture to me yet—they were just information, you get it? Like a squirrel, I put it all in my pouch and just gathered and gathered and gathered.

"And then I came, after Egypt's death, and said, 'What does she do at night?' And so the nation itself, like the person at the end of a life—see, it had, as we French say, 'a *double-entendre,*' for it was the life of twelve hours of the day and it was the life of an entire nation for five thousand years—was what I had in mind, while I was doing these hours as best I could.

"Then we came to their ideas of immortality. And, incidentally, I want you to make it possible for me to do that trial scene again sometime. We're so full of trials in our television nowadays—we can't think of anything better to do than a new form of trial—so while it's still raging, let's do the trial scene of Osiris, because I think, dramatically, with real figures, as it were, from five thousand years ago, would be something to offer.

"Telling it very briefly, when the curtain went up on the twelve hours of the night, supposedly at six o'clock where it took up with the death of Egypt at six—granted that she got up at six o'clock in the morning and *got* to work!—that when she got to six o'clock at night, and the curtain goes up, and you have this enormous set—and, incidentally, I have a kind of elephant grateful mind and I do remember things that have been done for me and I do remember an Egyptian play by Sir Beerbohm Tree, who is remembered for *Chu Chin Chow*. But this was a play about Akhenaton, the heretic pharaoh. And in one scene, these pillars, these gray-green pillars, started—and I'm at a matinee in London—and they went up and up and up into infinity, and you never saw anything so high in an enormous theater, His Majesty's, and way, way at the back was a little door. Now what part it played in the scene of his play, I wouldn't know, but it made an enormous impression on me.

"So when I came to *my* trial scene, I had gray-green, somber gray-green, and at the back were the knees of Osiris, and that was all that you saw. His knees were as high as the ceiling of the theater. So you can imagine the impression it made. Then, down two sides, are the forty-two judges of the dead. And I did them in staggered formation, like wings, so that there were twenty-one on this side and twenty-one on that, and these made the judges. You being the audience as the curtain went up, I was standing downstage in the same dress that I wore in life except that the wig and the dress and everything were green, pale ghostly green, so I looked the ghost of Egypt.

"In my hand was the little red heart. And she takes that and comes back and gives it to these animal gods near the knees of Osiris. One is Thoth, who is the scribe, and another one is Horus—maybe I've got my gods mixed now!—but anyway, he has the scales of justice, and then, alas and alack, there is this crocodile god over here, so you'd better watch your step! Anyway, she gives her heart to Horus and he holds it in his hand—he is going to put it in the other scale against the feather of truth, you get it?—and she makes her dance form, her actual choreography in our language of today, and what she said in dance form was 'I did not beat my slaves. I did not steal. I did not commit adultery, etc.' for forty-two sins. They allowed for quite a number in those days! . . . maybe more variety than we had, but it opens many possibilities of research! And so once that is finished, she waits, with her back to the audience, and stands there all trembling and awaits—of course with my Belasco lighting, you have seen her dancing for these judges—but suddenly everything goes down except the light on the scales. Naturally, I had a bead of light on me, and then there is a tremendous pause, and of course I pass—what would you expect me to do?—and the minute I do, and the scales even up, and I have protested my innocence, and I am innocent, and with that, there is a shout in the orchestra and it began to roar, and with that, I ran from the footlights right through the legs of Osiris.

"There was a door, like an old-fashioned dining-room swinging door that you just did *that* to and it opened. The backdrop went up slowly and I am now seen on the boat of Ra going into the 'Elysian Fields.' So that's the end of my trial scene. So that's what the Poster did to me, Walter."

How did she determine the style of movement to be used? "The bas-reliefs and the paintings." She knew, of course, that the Egyptians did not dance as the highly stylized, profiled, elongated ("they were all as skinny as a pencil!") figures would seem to suggest. So she selected the best poses, the most meaningful ones, and took it from there. At that time, in the creating of new movements never before seen, she did not even think of her old Delsarte exposures, with the zones of the body reflecting the physical, the emotional, and the spiritual areas of consciousness—the application of Delsarte was to come later, after her marriage to Shawn. With *Egypta,* she was wholly an expressive dancer, there was nothing psychological about her movement motivations. If she wanted to express sorrow, say, she went ahead and expressed it in what she considered natural movements. But although she was basically expressional, creating by impulse and instinct, there was a distinct pattern to her approach to choreography.

In a certain scene, for example, she would want a character to say "No!" in terms of gesture. With a natural movement, she would express this, and then say, "But how would the Egyptians say it?" Quite literally, then, she took these and other expressive actions and *translated* them into Egyptian, or what she thought would be the way that the ancient Egyptians spoke with their bodies.

The creative sequence in everything she did went something like this: first she had the *idea;* next the *way* of expressing it; and then, ultimately, the *character,* the *scene,* the *civilization,* the *period* or *era* in that specific culture. This was the evolution she followed throughout her career.

"*Ishtar,*" she said, "was the hardest, because there is so little of it. I even got down to coins, the size of your thumb, to find a little headdress, to find a particular action with a sistrum or something of the sort. This research was most difficult; perhaps they have more on Babylonian art and culture today, but then, forty years ago, there was very little.

"In everything I did, I first got the emotional impact of what I wanted to say—that has been basic all my life. I don't get the articulation *from* the art; I *use* the articulation of both sculpture and painting when I know what I want to do with it. Then if I cannot speak it correctly, in the movement sense, I will spend six weeks hunting up a particular gesture until I'm justified in using that gesture, justified in that it is authentic and can be properly included in my total plan of expression."

Egypta was enormously expensive and what it took in at the box office could not pay off its costs. After a series of matinees at the New Amsterdam Theater, St. Denis took to the road with excerpts from *Egypta* and, of course, her East Indian dances. *Egypta* itself was far too big (in those days) to tour—all her life, St. Denis had difficulty in adapting her grand production concepts to the practicalities of touring—for it consisted of five great scenes: (1) The Invocation to the Nile, with an outside temple setting and St. Denis as the personification of the river itself. (2) The Palace Dance, in which she, and others, dance for Pharaoh and his consort in a vast banquet hall. (3) The Veil of Isis, inside the temple, with St. Denis as the goddess who comes to life. (4) The Dance of Day takes place on the plains of Ra, and from dawn to sunset, the life of Egypt is unfolded in terms of tilling the soil, tending livestock, fishing, hunting, weaving, training for battle, promoting the arts, submitting to invasion, the conquest, and the dying, with shifting lighting effects reflecting the course of the sun over a day and over an age. (5) The Dance of Night takes place in the great judgment hall of Osiris. And this is the scene which St. Denis described in detail on the tape recording made a half century after the last performance of the full-length *Egypta*.

Egypta ended its only Broadway run December 30, 1910. In January 1911 it was given in Boston, and then it was broken up into serviceable touring dances.

The tour really got under way with a two-week stand in Chicago and carried her throughout the Middle West and the Rocky Mountain States to California. The most important stop of all—although she didn't know it at the time—was at the Broadway Theater in Denver, Colorado (March 20–25, 1911). A divinity student attended one of these performances. Years later, he wrote: "I had seen the Russians a few months before, and although I marveled, they had awakened nothing deep in me. But when I saw *The Incense* I wept—not caring that it was in a crowded theater—and never before, or since, have I known so true a religious experience or so poignant a revelation of perfect beauty. I date my own artistic birth from that night." The twenty-year-old was Ted Shawn.

He had just seen a great star, a great artist, a woman he knew was a pioneer, a spiritual figure he sensed must be a prophet. Nine years later, his words were incorporated into the first of many books, *Ruth St. Denis: Pio-*

neer and Prophet, lavishly produced in only a few hundred copies (one volume text, one volume photographs) for fifty dollars and now a collectors' item.

Ruth Dennis and Ruth St. Denis had attracted simple farm boys, sophisticated New Yorkers, French sculptors, Viennese poets, producers, architects, nobles, and ordinary citizens, so she illumined a college boy among many college boys. But Edwin Myers Shawn was special; he didn't know it at the time, but he sensed, as did Isadora Duncan and Ruth St. Denis, an inexorable march toward destiny.

His mother, who died when he was a lad, belonged to the great Booth family of actors; his father was a successful and respected newspaperman; his inner self sought for some kind of way, not yet within his ken, that would relate his spiritual compulsions to some kind of performing. Preaching, of course, was the answer. The family, including his stepmother, whom he adored, was a trifle surprised when he failed to outgrow a boyish interest in a life of church service, but they went along with it. Later, they would respect his abdication from pulpit for the stage. What triggered the change was a desperate, almost fatal, illness.

He had been born in Kansas City, Missouri (October 21, 1891) but he grew up in Denver, Colorado, where he subsequently enrolled at the University of Denver. He was big and husky—180 to 185 pounds was a comfortable weight throughout his career—and heavy work in a sawmill added muscles to the frame.

It was in his junior year that he contracted diphtheria.

The serum that saved his life, however, paralyzed him from the waist down, and for more than a year he was bedridden in a hospital. Therapy of mind, as well as of body, was called for. Painfully, remorselessly, he got muscles to feel, to quiver, and finally to move. When he could, he turned to increasingly complex exercises, and finally to dance lessons. His mind went along with his body, and as he has often said, "I danced my way out of the church and into the theater. Ruth danced her way from theater to church. And our lives came together."

His first dance teacher was Hazel Wallack, who had performed with the Metropolitan Opera Ballet. Her training was, of course, classical dance, and as a discipline it was of enormous value to the convalescent, but as an art form, it did not answer the needs of a questing, questioning mind. He and Hazel, to whom he became engaged (his third romance!), were participants in a charity affair for which they performed an exhibition ballroom dance. But charity or no, all hell broke loose, for a photograph in the newspaper showed Miss Wallack's leg, due to a slit skirt, up to the knee! The chancellor of the university informed the former divinity student that he wished he were still enrolled so that he could have the pleasure of expelling him! A fraternity brother, on learning that the youth who was to become the University of Denver's most famous dropout was determined to make dance his life's work, said quite simply, and with utter conviction, "But Ted, *men* don't dance." When the newcomer to dance scholarliness pointed out that in most world societies men were the chief dancers, the college chum agreed that it was all right for pagans, and maybe even for Russians, but not for Americans!

Ted Shawn went ahead with his plans for an unprecedented career in the world of American dance. He had his dreams, even images of what he would do. He saw Ruth St. Denis and his vision was affirmed. She was dancing about the spirit, about deity, about the God deep within. She had found a new dance—or rediscovered ancient dance motivations—and he would have to do the same for a man. Reluctantly, but inevitably, he had to break with Hazel, for ballet was not to be his avenue of dance. He left Denver for California, for Los Angeles, where some of the greatests performers in the world were gathered for the art of performing, for the great creative surge of motion pictures. But in this creative pattern there was almost no dance, and Ted Shawn, instead of finding a dance master, became one himself for a new dance age.

Separately from his idol, St. Denis, he began making a dance name for himself. It never entered his head that he, building a fine reputation in Southern California, would ever meet the international dance star whose first home was New York's Broadway and whose other homes were Berlin, Paris, London, Vienna. She, in turn, had never heard of him. From the time he saw her dance in 1911, three years were to pass before there would transpire a meeting clearly destined to change the course of two volatile lives, dance in America, the theater in America, and dancing aorund the world.

CHAPTER VII

Despite the losses incurred by *Egypta,* Harris was not only willing but eager to produce two more dance dramas for St. Denis. One was *O-mika,* a Japanese dance play (in it, St. Denis was frequently referred to as an "actress"), and *Bakawali, A Hindu Love Tale of Indra's Heavenly Court.* Both were inspired by stories written by the famous and popular American expatriate, Lafcadio Hearn. The former stemmed from Hearn's "A Legend of Fugen-Bosatsu"; the latter, from "Stray Leaves from Strange Literature."

In 1900 St. Denis, in a quick trip from London to Paris before returning to America with *Zaza,* had not only seen Loie Fuller but also, in the Fuller theater, a Mme Sadi Yaco, a Japanese actress-dancer. The performance made a great impression on her, for the subtlety, the underplaying, the delicacy were quite the reverse of the flamboyance associated with ballet or show-business dancing. During her three-year tour of Europe, she experimented, on one occasion, with a dance on a Japanese theme, but it was not until *O-mika,* presented at the Fulton Theater in New York in the spring of 1913, that her long-time and cumulative fascination with things Japanese bore its finest fruit.

When the 1911–12 concert tour had brought her to California, she had an opportunity to study, on a daily basis, with a geisha instructor, she saw some Noh dramas, and she became acquainted with Americans who had lived and studied in Japan. All of this provided her with the vast amount of research material she always required. In addition, of course, she haunted museums and galleries, studied Japanese painting and costuming, listened to Japanese speech, song, and instrumental music.

When she returned to New York, she and Harris planned to have *O-mika* ready for Broadway by the spring of 1913. Disaster, however, struck from a wholly unexpected and melodramatic source. As *O-mika* was in rehearsal and production in 1912, Harris, returning from a trip to Europe, went down in the tragic sinking of the *Titanic.* This not only represented a terrible personal loss to St. Denis, who had found Harris a devoted friend as well as a generous and believing producer of her dance theater, but it also left her, for the moment, without the financial backing she needed to get *O-mika* onto the stage.

By going deeply into debt, and with insufficient promotion to launch the new enterprise properly, she opened March 11, 1913, to critical acclaim but a disastrous box office.

The dance drama itself—and it was a play with dancing—was richly costumed and lavishly staged. Its theme was that of a search for truth, for goodness, for revelation, and its simple hero, a Buddhist monk, was guided by a vision to the house of courtesans where he was tempted, revolted, and confused until, in a brilliant transformation scene, he learned his lesson, that God is everywhere, and that *O-mika,* once the trappings of her trade fell away, was an incarnation of deity.

St. Denis used the ancient devices of the Japanese theater—a thread is pulled and an entire costume falls away to reveal another dress—to effect the transformation in an era when America had never seen such theatrical magic. Furthermore, she spoke in *O-mika* and learned her lines phonetically, and so perfectly did she master an alien tongue that a Japanese came back stage at one performance and gave her an English translation of what she had said!

In *Radha,* the priests had intoned; in *The Yogi,* there had, in the Vienna staging, been chanting; in *The Cobras* and *The Nautch,* the passers-by, and the rajahs had used dialogue and St. Denis herself had spoken a phrase or two. But in *O-mika* she was again an actress as well as a dancer. With Brother, whom she coaxed into the assignment, she did the big samurai war dance, a far cry from her usual lyricism, and as she was viewed by a reporter for the Japan Society in New York, she was so perfect that she was actually urged to go to Japan to reinstill the beauty of classical Japanese performing into the spirits of the Japanese themselves. Indeed, the Japanese *Times* said: "We have nothing but praise and admiration for the part this famous actress played. The grace of her movement, the delicacy of her touch . . . the refined taste . . . the inborn beauty of the actress . . ." And she was referred to as an actress because in Japan, acting without dance, or dance without drama, would be unthinkable.

In later years, Japan itself took her to its heart, and in India, she was written about in Sanscrit and credited, on more than one occasion, with restoring India's confidence and faith in its own dance heritage.

O-mika, with a score by Robert Hood Bowers, was staged with the following dances: "The Dance of the Flower Arrangement," "The Chrysanthemum Dance," "The Dance of the Thirteenth-Century Poetess," "The Samurai Dance," "The Dance of Fugen-Bosatsu."

Bakawali had music by Arthur Nevin, but it also made use of the spoken word. It included "The Dance of the Gold and Black Sari" (the ancestor of the much later solo, *Dance of the Black and Gold Sari,* to music of Stoughton), "Dance of the Blue Flame," "Jewel Dance Before the God of Heaven," and "Dance in the Forest of Ceylon."

Both *O-mika* and *Bakawali,* because of the Broadway losses, did not survive as a dual bill of dance dramas, but excerpts from them became popular items in St. Denis's touring repertory for vaudeville, concert, and society appearances.

In fact, these were lean years, and the dancer found it necessary to revert to the patronage of society bigwigs. Her route lists, her diaries, her recollections attest to this. The situation did not mean that she was not honored, not respected. To the contrary, her creations added to her stature as a major American artist. But without Harris to guide her, she made errors in judgment, and, of course, the first flush of novelty had worn off. Except in matters of income, popularity by itself did not interest her, and the income mattered only because it allowed her to create what she felt compelled to do.

Once, well past middle age, she returned to one of her favorite cities, Boston. She was booked to appear in a small concert hall that seated about four hundred. Just a few years before, she had played a theater that seated close to two thousand. She felt no discouragement at all. With great simplicity, she said, "It doesn't matter about the size of the audience. I have *performed* for thousands when they found me exotic, the vogue, daring, but I have *danced,* at any given time, for about ten people. They are the ones that saw something more than a novelty, something more than surface. They were the ones I reached. They were the ones that left the theater forever different from the way they were when they came in. All of my long, long life, I have danced for those ten."

To have business acumen and to keep in fashion were essential to a successful theater life. Brother and Mother St. Denis (they, too, accepted the canonization from plain Dennis) did their best to manage the business life of their adored maverick. But something new was happening to dance itself. Diaghilev and his Ballet Russe had given ballet a rebirth in Paris the very year that St. Denis, in triumph, returned to America. Before the Diaghilev troupe got to America, Gertrude Hoffman mounted three unauthorized stagings of Fokine ballets, just as earlier she had taken St. Denis innovations and used them in vaudeville acts. But the ballet impact meant that something new had come to the world of dance in provincial America, the male dancer. Nijinsky had electrified Paris. The Hoffman prevue had used men dancers. The day of male roles being done *en travesti* was over.

In the field of popular dance, the male was essential. Who could go ballroom dancing without a partner? An English boy and an American girl took this simple notion and turned it into a world-wide dance craze. They were the Castles, Vernon and Irene. Everyone identified with them, for they popularized not only special dances (the maxixe, the Castle walk, etc.) but dancing itself. They made it fashionable. With the Castles in the air, with the burst of ballet males, Ruth St. Denis, lone lady, needed a partner. She had had men in her company from the very start of her career as an artist, but she needed Karsavina's equivalent to Nijinsky, Irene's equivalent to Vernon. She knew it. She determined to find a partner, and if not exactly a partner, a male to participate in her theater of dance. Ted Shawn was more than ready. Indeed, he already had a head start.

When he left the university, Denver, Hazel, the fraternity, the formal church, he headed for Los Angeles, but he was prudent enough to have a homely craft at his disposal. He could type. And type he did, for a salary, in Los Angeles' water works department. The inexorable drive that was to make Ted Shawn a major force not only in American dance but in the world's dance was already at work.

He rented a studio where he gave social dancing lessons and where he rehearsed and experimented with the still fuzzy ideas of the dance art he hoped to create. At this time, he met Norma Gould, a ballet dancer who also had a school, and together they started their own *thé dansant* series in Los Angeles. They called these "tango teas" and they became enormously popular. Indeed, the names of Ted Shawn and Norma Gould became well known in the entire area.

Shawn, reminiscing, has marveled at the endurance and resilience of youth, for in those days not only did he work long hours for the water company, and by scrimping on his lunch hour, finish in time for the daily "tango teas," but following the teas, he would rush to his studio where he taught the popular ballroom dances and then race back to join Norma for after-theater entertaining in the famous Alexandria Hotel! Weekends simply made for a tighter schedule. Furthermore, dances had to be choreographed for that time when he could get away from the social dances, which held little interest for him other than the money they brought in. And that money wasn't being built up to spend on a concert of his own or, perhaps, with Norma; it was there, and growing, in order to pay for studies elsewhere, perhaps even in distant New York. For he still thought of himself as a student preparing himself to serve a great art that had fallen on lean days, except for St. Denis and Duncan.

He was, of course, in movieland, or in the primitive beginnings of what was to become the motion picture capital of the world. Edison, who had invented the new medium, was there and eager for experiments in filming. For Edison, he wrote a script, which he has described as "slim," and created the dances for an historically remarkable movie called *Dance of the Ages*. It started out with primitive man and how he danced—or how Ted *thought* he danced—and in a matter of minutes had streaked through history to the kind of dances he and Norma were doing at their "tango teas." In no time, in the light of swift cinematic advances, such a film became obsolete, but looking at it from the vantage point of more than half a century later, it returns to our heritage as a surprisingly inventive adventure into cinematography in dance terms. The entire film, not feature length but fairly elaborate in production terms, was shot in two weeks, with Ted, Norma, and some dancers they had assembled.

In fact, there was a little company in the making, and when Shawn heard that the Santa Fe Railroad was engaging entertainers to provide diversion for employees and workers of all sorts along the Santa Fe route, he urged Norma to join him for a cross-country junket that would get them to New York, all fares (round-trip) paid. Solo acts had gone out before, but the suggestion of a dance-music ensemble of six caught the fancy of the authorities and the Shawn-Gould unit headed out for a transcontinental tour. They were billed as "interpretive" dancers and publicized with the accent on elegance. What actually happened was far from elegant. In Gallup, New Mexico, they performed under conditions that included inadequate lighting, a much too small dancing area, and for the males in the group, a dressing room which was nothing more than an emptied swimming pool!

They finally made it to New York City where Shawn and Gould were determined to study. The first port of call, oddly enough, was not New York itself but, rather, a rural Connecticut town about forty miles away, New Canaan.

Here he was exposed to Delsarte—somewhat watered down and adapted—for the first time. He did not know it was Delsarte, for the name of the enterprise was the Uni-Trinian School of Personal Harmonizing and Self-Development. Ted had heard about it through an article by Bliss Carman, the poet, who had made some comments about dance which intrigued the avid young student. An exchange of letters led to enrollment at the school, which was headed by Mary Perry King and located in Sunshine House, owned by Dr. and Mrs. King. Carman was their protegé. (Incidentally, her summer home in the mountains on the other side of the Hudson River was named "Moonshine.")

Ted, Norma, and one of the girls of their group worked long hours daily for one month with Mrs. King. They did her exercises, her studies in rhythm, and even her choreography, which Ted found much too feminine for him. They were even required to wear the Tri-Unian shoes, with a curved sole like a rocking chair, which Mrs. King had invented in order to achieve what she thought was a rolling, rhythmic gait.

Sadder, wiser, but often tortured by stifled laughter, they stuck it out and then returned to New York for much study and some performing. Shawn took classes in ballet, in Spanish dance, and brought himself up to date on the newest ballroom forms. He hired studios, taught classes, and he and Gould had some successful engagements in and around New York. But he was determined, if at all possible, to have some lessons in Oriental dance from the greatest artist of them all, Ruth St. Denis. He did not even know if she taught, or would teach, anyone except members of her company, but he thought he would ask. One of his own pupils was going to a gathering at the St. Denis studio and agreed to ask the star if she would be interested in having a new pupil who admired her extravagantly and would pay handsomely for the privilege of studying with her. The message was delivered, Brother St. Denis was dispatched to look over the applicant. He passed muster and in due course was invited to have tea with her in her town house close to Riverside Drive. (When she first returned from Europe, she had bought a country house at Prince's Bay, Staten Island, where Mother, Father, Buzz, and herself might feel that they had recaptured something that had been missing since they lost Pin Oaks. Half brother Tom, his wife and children, lived near by. The trip to Manhattan for rehearsals, performing, and other business turned out to be too much for St. Denis, so she eventually secured her five-story house in Manhattan.)

Ted was not the first young male dancer that St. Denis auditioned; he was the last. She had sent out a call for men dancers because of the financial failure of *Egypta* and *O-mika,* and because her tours of the extracts from these great works and even the Indian dances were not drawing as they should. She recognized the Castle craze, that everyone wanted to see someone really professional do, say, the *maxixe.* She was disheartened by the trend, and she wondered, deep within, if her vision of dance beauty would survive. A southern tour was booked and the pressures of advice were such that she half-convinced herself that some example of modern ballroom dance must be on her programs, although she later expressed the opinion that a troupe of trained monkeys would have been just as suitable, and perhaps even more so!

In Shawn's book, *One Thousand and One Night Stands* (written with Gray Poole), he tells of how he waited, with a combination of fear and anticipation, in her studio in the Riverside house. He had fallen under her spell in 1911 in Denver. This was New York City, 1914. Restlessly, he paced the room, looking at the photographs of Ruth St. Denis in a variety of roles. Nowhere did he see a portrait of Ruth St. Denis the woman. He was curious about the woman behind the goddess. All he knew was that she wore tailored suits and had prematurely white hair. "My reverie," he writes, "was interrupted by a thumping and clop-clopping on the stairs high up in the house. Rudely brought to myself, I thought 'Not even a cook or an old aunt should stomp about like that in the home of Ruth St. Denis.' The weighted footsteps came nearer, the studio door swung open, and Ruth herself entered. I'm positive that my jaw literally sagged. My immediate shock was at once magically dispelled and forgotten as the radiant personality of St. Denis engulfed me.

"On sight we began to talk. The conversation we started then was continuous through our years of touring and has been interrupted only at semicolons by geographical separations. That day, in the spring of 1914, we talked from teatime until Ruth asked me to stay for dinner, through dinner until well after midnight when I asked what time we might meet later in the morning of the same day."

He returned with costumes for a Greek ("pseudo," as he described it), Slavic, and an Aztec dagger dance. The great star lavished him with praise, and her family concurred. The following day, he was back again to learn if she would accept him as a pupil. She was not there; instead, he was directed to Brother's office where Brother St. Denis, "then business manager for his sister, asked me to join the St. Denis company as Ruth's dancing partner. Dazed, amazed, and shaken, I managed to gasp an enthusiastic 'Yes.' "

St. Denis in her autobiography mused upon the restless days of self-search in the Riverside studio: "I had paid my most constant service to the other gods of my idolatry. I had brought my adoration to the feet of

Beauty and Wisdom, but now my god of love, so long neglected, was commanding my presence in his sanctuary on pain of death of all progress and all joy. For does not wisdom spring from Love and is Beauty not the very form of Desire? Fragments of old assurances came to my mind as I sat there. 'Before thou speakest, I will answer.' Within ten days Ted Shawn stood in this same room."

The days passed, and he came. "His eyes were beautiful and boyish and full of charm. I felt his latent strength even before he danced, and then at once I knew . . . the fact that I allowed him to stay until midnight shows how attractive I found this boy to be . . . when he did his *Dagger Dance* at the audition, I exclaimed, 'This is the best male dancing material in America!' I knew that if I were going to have a man dancer on my program this was the one man in America I would choose."

Ten days later, Ruth St. Denis and her company, with Ted Shawn, set out on tour. For some long-forgotten reason, Mother, the protector, did not make the tour, and that was the hand of fate at work. Their first stage appearance together was in Paducah, April 13, 1914. And it was in Paducah that the romance began to flower. The talking, the exchange of ideas, the dreams continued and exploded. There was theater and, together, escape from the theater. The goddess of dancing, so often tempted by earthly love, so often the one who would invite masculine ardor only to dismiss it sadly but peremptorily, was beginning to find herself as a woman, maternal at first and then, submissive (but very briefly) to an ardent youth fired with both her image and herself.

She was lost but on the brink of discovering, uncertain and fearful but desirous, demanding, and at the same time, needing desperately. The mere thought of marriage was repugnant. And yet? With her deep religious convictions, she knew that she could not accept being a mistress. She pondered seriously on Isadora Duncan, whom she admired with an esthetic devotion she offered no other dancer. She understood the wild spirit that made Isadora defy convention and proudly bear her cherished children out of wedlock. In essence, Ruth St. Denis was the same, for she did not want to be trapped by convention, bridled by legal marriage laws, subject to the conventions which prevailed from New Jersey to California. And yet . . . and yet . . . the Puritan was within her. She needed Love (capitalized), and she needed to preserve the image of spiritual dedication, of a sophisticated virginity which had disturbed, startled, and electrified the theater. She compromised.

On August 13, 1914, Ruth St. Denis and Ted Shawn were married. She refused to wear a wedding ring—she thought of it as a "band" rather than jewelry—and she refused to say "obey" in the vows.

Later she wrote, "He was, and always remained, an adorable lover."

But if the marriage itself was ever tempestuous, as well as physically ecstatic, the courtship combined poetry and philosophy with wild melodrama. Before he could capture Ruthie as his own, young Ted Shawn had to face a raging, protective matriarch, Mother, who was not about to let her kitten find a mate.

A battle raged.

Mother lost.

CHAPTER VIII

On this first tour, the new lovers were joyously savoring courtship together or, when briefly separated by previous booking commitments, exchanging impassioned letters. This seemed to be *it* for the youth who had had three major sweethearts (one of them, Hazel, an official fiancée), and for the great star sought after by White, Belasco, Hofmannsthal, Rodin, and even by a young man who got her to meet him in Italy for what was presumably an assignation but from which she departed without doing more than stroking his hair in the twilight.

This time, would it work? Her newest suitor had determination as well as ardor. With her, he was in ecstasy, and away from her he pined, quite literally, with loss of weight, color, and vitality. She responded with equal enthusiasm, but she was uncertain. She remembered her friend Lizzie, and the terrifying image of marriage which she had carried all these years. Mother was her protector, Buzz was her off-stage boss and buddy. Did she need anyone else? She knew she did, but with a curious prescience, she was aware that she, and Ted, would have to pay, and dearly, for their union. She hesitated, procrastinated. Finally, she said "Yes." And then Ted had to deal with Mother. It was a confrontation. The strong woman who had kept a family together, held to a brilliant but improvident husband, guided a son, and directed the course of a dazzling career, did her best to avert what she genuinely believed would be disaster. She pled, threatened, stormed, cajoled, explained, and reasoned—all against the marriage—but to no avail. And so, after exhausting hours of a battle of wills, she surrendered. She also gave her blessing to the match, and a piece of advice: "I respect your young man, so if you must, marry him. But I warn you, he's no weakling." Ted Shawn was not a weakling, as his bride found out. They were married August 13, 1914, in a civil service in New York City, and later in a religious ceremony. For fifteen years they lived together as man and wife—they were never divorced—and during that time they made dance history in their own land and around the world.

The premarital tour took them through the South, and young Ted, aside from doing some solos derived from the Shawn-Gould tour and later experiments, provided St. Denis with the popular ballroom dances that she had forlornly felt were important to her bookings. His partner was Hilda Beyer, a charming girl, with whom he had such success that they were engaged for some dates separate from those with St. Denis. In later seasons, St. Denis herself appeared with her husband in exhibition ballroom dances.

Less then a week after St. Denis, following much vacillating, said to her wooer, "Well, let's get it over with!" and headed for the marriage license bureau, they were off on a tour of one-night stands that would last for more than six months. If anyone wondered, on looking at a program, about a relationship between the star, Ruth St. Denis, and a supporting dancer listed as René St. Denis, investigation would have proved that Brother, or "B.," with no given name, had adopted one. And nobody, in 1914, knew the relationship of Ruth St. Denis and Ted Shawn, for they had been married under their own names: Ruth Dennis and Edwin Myers Shawn. It was Ruth's idea to keep the whole arrangement a secret. Sometime later, in Ted's home town of Kansas City, which had not received his return as a dancer with any favorite-son kudos, Ruthie confided her blissful married state to a charming, sensitive woman. She also happened to be a newspaper reporter. St. Denis knew this but, somehow, felt that she was simply engaged in girl-to-girl confidences. In hours, America read, in great headlines, that: "RUTH ST. DENIS MARRIES TED SHAWN, THE MOST BEAUTIFUL MAN IN THE WORLD." The appellation was somewhat off, for although Shawn was good-looking, no one had ever thought of him, St. Denis, possibly, excepted, as beautiful. There was, in those days, a much admired vaudeville star, Paul Swan, who was billed as

"The Most Beautiful Man in the World." And he was just that, with a perfect body and a face that possessed the features of a classical Greek statue. Somewhere along the line, a reporter or an editor confused Swan and Shawn. It took Ted years to live it down.

After Ted entered Ruth's life with such impact, the role of Mother dwindled—her daughter had a new protector. But Mother, as she was almost always called, not only by her family but by dancers who came to know her, had been all-important to the career of Ruth St. Denis. She was an intellectual, spiritual, and disciplinary force in the life of a child-girl-woman genius. In a way, she was a critic, for if she clucked over her Ruthie, she also expected perfection from her on stage, if nowhere else. Both Ted and Brother recall that when St. Denis had given a performance which had received tumultuous response, Mother would nod sagely and say that it was "about eighty per cent" good but that there was twenty per cent room for improvement. Mother remained an important being for as long as she lived, but the need for her drew to a close on that fateful day in 1914 when the daughter found her mate.

Brother, too, had been of inestimable importance to his sister's career—he had created for her lighting effects which had never before existed in the theater, and lighting was more important to her than music; he was an easy-going chaperon when Mother was off on business or at home with Mr. Dennis, and he was, in a real sense, a boon companion. So he, too, in 1914, knew that his sister could get along without him, for Ted was there.

But where Mother's life was heading into its evening, Brother's was just beginning. He did the 1914–15 tour, which he *thought* would be his last, although a much later reunion with his sister and her husband would change his life once again. Meanwhile, a family of his own, studies of his own choosing, and an independent career were first in his mind. He had recently married Emily Purkis, and the two of them had been the only attendants at the secret St. Denis-Shawn nuptuals. Oddly enough, Emily had been a wardrobe mistress in a theater across the street from the theater where St. Denis had been playing in London some years before, but Buzz did not meet her then. They met in America, where Emily was working in her theater wardrobe capacity. As with Ruthie's marriage, there were some family doubts about Buzz and Emily, but they themselves had none at all and quite literally lived happily ever after until Emily St. Denis's death in the fall of 1968, only a few weeks after her world-famous sister-in-law had died. She bore two handsome sons and lived to see them happily married and with children of their own.

Brother, who had enjoyed the theater life with Ruth and had earned some recognition not only as a lighting expert but also as a dancer (the spear dance in *O-mika* and ballroom dances in the 1914–15 tour)—in 1969 he proudly recalled, "I played the Palace in New York"— kept on with dancing in vaudeville for a few seasons, after realizing that a strong-willed Shawn and a male St. Denis would have disagreements about stagings.

In due course, he departed from his sister's artistic

bent and headed into his father's area of science. He went to school, to Columbia University, where he studied geology, with an eye to specializing in oil geology. On his first major ''detecting" job, he and a partner-geologist recommended a site in Wyoming. Brother recalls that he did the "original work" on the analysis of the oil potential, and that "oil came in at 4,000 barrels a day." With understandable pride, he said in 1969, as a gentleman in his eighties, "and it's been coming in ever since. From that one oil field, I've received an income for more than forty years! It's still producing!" This was quite an advance for the kid who used to visit his father at the Brooklyn Navy Yard and scrounge brass scraps which he could sell for three dollars a haul.

In 1969, alert, active, happy to go out skeet-shooting with a grandson, he took note of the disorders on college campuses and said, "I think I was wise to go to Columbia University in 1920 instead of now!"

It would seem, then, that Brother St. Denis leaves the picture. He never does, for he was back with his sister and with Ted for an unprecedented and never again equaled tour in the mid-1920's, and he was there with love and money to give Ruthie a home, a studio, a center in her beloved California Hills for the long last years of her life.

Brother made a fortune in oil. He also made a fortune in another enterprise, one that stemmed directly from his sister and her husband. But that comes much later in the story of Ruth St. Denis.

*　　　*　　　*

Personal romance to the contrary, Ruth St. Denis's romance with the theater never faltered. Before they were married, two new solos, both in artistic gestation for a time, came into her repertory. One was *The Legend of the Peacock,* a tale of Moslem origin, in which she played a vain and greedy East Indian girl of great beauty and cruel ambition who was transformed into a peacock. Both as a solo and as a dance within a "scene," *The Peacock* was a huge success with audiences. A rather well-known painting of her in the role, by Robert Henri, attests to the appeal which the work had with artists as well as with the general public. The music, by Edmund Roth, was composed on an occasion when St. Denis was organizing improvisations, begun in 1909 in London, into some sort of form. *Peacock* remained within her repertory for most of her life.

A dance quite literally born of improvisation, *The Scherzo Waltz,* with music by McNair Ilgenfritz, who composed it while she danced in her studio, was on the bill at Ravinia Park on the brief tour that preceded the marriage. In it, she wore a short tunic, showed her own white hair (held in place by a kind of turban) for the first time on stage, and danced movements which had nothing whatever to do with the Orient. Indeed, she had often been described in the press as one who was "primarily a gestural dancer" and one not noted "for elaborate foot work." *The Scherzo Waltz* was her good-humored answer to those who thought of her as langorous. It had force and thrust to it from the point of view of body dynamics, and there were also the old vaudeville tricks, among them, the kicking of the back of her head. Not long after, she added an *Impromptu,* which included a cakewalk strut, as a sort of encore for *Scherzo.* This she danced to music of Victor Herbert ("Al Fresco") and what she did on stage was literally a matter of the moment.

The Scherzo Waltz and the *Impromptu* were intended to be light and fun. There were times when they were funny. St. Denis, in later years, used to chuckle over an incident involving them. A mayor, having seen a picture of the costume and on learning, somehow, that Ruth St. Denis was barelegged and wore no "fleshings," threatened that if she appeared in his fair city in such undress, he would have her arrested and carted off to jail. Since fleshings, at a distance, look like flesh, as they were supposed to, St. Denis could not see how it mattered, morally, whether she wore them or not. She chose "not," and went on stage.

But she went on stage with full streetwear covering her *Scherzo* costume: hat, gloves, shoes, suit, furs, and all. She did the dance once through and, at certain moments, divested herself of an article of streetwear and tossed it at the mayor in the audience. Finally, she got down to the costume itself, and repeated the entire dance to storms of applause and approval and to the chagrin of the totally defeated mayor. "I guess," she said years later, "I could claim to be the mother, or grandmother, of the striptease!"

In February 1915, Ruth St. Denis and Ted Shawn produced their first joint choreography, *The Garden of*

Kama, in San Francisco. Their first duet had been in a suite of Arabic dances, later titled *Ourieda, A Romance of the Desert,* at Chicago's Ravinia Park in the summer of 1914. But *The Garden of Kama,* an East Indian dance drama suggested by a theme from Lawrence Hope's "Indian Love Lyrics," with music by Stoughton, represented their first major production. At almost the same time that this initial union of talents took place, another union, an unforeseen union of names, occurred.

On their touring program, they danced together the inescapable exhibition ballroom dance offering, in this case, something called *The St. Denis Mazurka.* For promotion purposes, the manager of a theater in Portland, Oregon, thought it would be a good idea to have a contest to select a name, possibly involving Portland, for this Ruth St. Denis-Ted Shawn duet. The prize was to be eight box seats in the theater. Ruth and Ted went over the entries, discarding like mad. Then they stopped short: *The Denishawn Rose Mazurka.* The "rose" was included, of course, since Portland was known as "The City of Roses." Margaret Ayer was the winner. Nobody knows whether she ever used the seats herself, for she never went backstage, St. Denis and Shawn never met her, and yet she invented the name that made dance history all over the country, all over the world.

Shawn had professional dance roots in California, and St. Denis took California to her heart and kept it there until she died. Indeed, the Denis clan went West. Mother, who had stayed on, lonely and sad, in the house near Riverside Drive, came West to live near her daughter. Mr. Dennis came, too, and as a proud veteran of the Civil War, ended his days nearby in a comfortable home for those old soldiers who had served their country well. Brother, of course, came many years later, but when he did, he and Emily and the boys made Los Angeles their home.

It was in Los Angeles that Denishawn, as a school, was born, later to give its name to the companies of Ruth St. Denis and Ted Shawn and to the dance schools, worthy of their patronage, which sprang up coast to coast.

In the summer of 1967, a ninety-year-old lady held up her expressive hands, the hands that poets had praised, and with a tiny gesture said, "Denishawn was born as a little pamphlet *this* size." And so it was.

It was inevitable that a new dance school come into being to serve the needs of a new dance age. Shawn had had a successful school in Los Angeles, and St. Denis had done some teaching of a rather desultory nature, but this new school, which at first did not use the Denishawn name, was to bring to the classroom the tools of two artists, the senior and the junior, the female and the male.

Because they were free spirits, they felt that the school itself should be unconfined by walls or old esthetic traditions. It was, then, out-of-doors. They had a floor put down on a tennis court, a tent-canopy over the top, and a cigar box served as the cash register where students dropped their money for classes. One dollar paid for lessons and lunch.

The classes themselves included ballet, Oriental, Span-

Above left: "The Peacock."
ARNOLD GENTHE, N. Y. *Right:* The
instinctive dancer. G. F. FOLEY, N.Y.
Below right: The matron, with
husband, Shawn. UNDERWOOD &
UNDERWOOD STUDIOS. *Left:* A portrait by Marcus Blechman who
made many photographs of the
dancer. MARCUS BLECHMAN

On the great Oriental tour (1925-1926). Shawn is second from left; St. Denis is third from right; Charles Weidman is far right. *Below:* "Home" to India.

"Ishtar of the Seven Gates."

"Dance of the Black and Gold Sari," a smash hit around the world. MARCUS BLECHMAN

"Josephine and Hippolyte," a love duet. The jewels worn by St. Denis actually belonged to the Empress Josephine.
SUNAMI

Perfection all the way.
SUNAMI

"Spirit of the Sea" in the sea itself.

"A Tagore Poem." 1926. SUNAMI

Denishawn House, Van Cortlandt Park, New York City (1927).
Oustide view. EDDOWES CO., INC., N.Y.

The great studio. EDDOWES CO., INC., N.Y.

"Jurgen," the controversial James Branch Cabell novel in dance form, with St. Denis and Shawn at Lewisohn Stadium (1929). The end of a marriage and a joint career was in sight.
TOWNSEND, N.Y.

The lonely years.
MARCUS BLECHMAN

Dancing in Riverside Church.
SUNAMI

Above: La Meri and Miss Ruth: together they founded the School of Natya. *Below:* Glamour in old age. LES CLARK

"The Yogi"—many years later.
CONSTANTINE

The actress again—this time in
"The Madwoman of Chaillot."

Above: The "Egyptian Ballet."

St. Denis and Shawn remember the thousands of performances they once did of the "Egyptian Ballet" and of "Jurgen."

PHOTOGRAPHS BY RADFORD BASCOME

"Jurgen."

America's Ruth St. Denis;
Europe's Mary Wigman.
Pioneers!

Dame Margot Fonteyn and Dame Ninette de Valois of Britain's Royal Ballet,
salute the First Lady of American Dance.

Top: Joseph Pilates (at 80), master body-builder, and one of his most famous pupils, St. Denis (at 84), at Jacob's Pillow. *Left:* Ted and Ruthie at Jacob's Pillow — the breach had been healed. *Right:* Looking toward "a more living life" at 80.

Near ninety—the body must be used and disciplined every day.

"White Jade"—in later years (1959). JACK MITCHELL

St. Denis and Shawn in
"Siddhas of the Upper Air."

Married for fifty years — St.
Denis and Shawn. JACK
MITCHELL

Dance and God's world.

The last years—home, near Brother, in Hollywood.

Miss Ruth, with her "beloved 'cricket'," on stage at New York's famous dance center at the YM-YWHA.

Miss Ruth, today and yesterday, at the Museum of the City of New York.

ish, basic movement exercises to prepare the body for dancing, and whatever other techniques and styles became available through guest teachers and instructors. As Shawn stated, "The dance is too big to be encompassed by any one system," and so they took the dances of the world and the dances of the ages as their concept of a curriculum. Technique instruction came mainly from Shawn; St. Denis taught certain Oriental techniques and she also lectured. Both were interested in finding specific talents in the individual, and often they diagnosed the capabilities of their students and tried to guide them into directions which seemed most suitable.

That their approach succeeded is clearly attested to by the results: Martha Graham, Doris Humphrey, Charles Weidman, those who became vaudeville and follies headliners, prominent teachers, a host of professional dancers, and a galaxy of movie stars whose careers were benefited by lessons at Denishawn.

Ted, as one might suppose, was the organizer, the real maker of the Denishawn School. Ruth was interested, even excited, mainly because her new lover-husband was charged with the idea of dance dissemination. But in the years ahead she would fight off the organization duties which Denishawn entailed, rebel briefly, escape, and return. Her feeling about her marriage followed a parallel course.

She was deeply, ardently in love with her man, but she continued to have the gnawing doubts, not about love but about marriage. She sensed that their marital union, no matter how blissful, had diverted them from their individual courses of creativity. In her mind, in doubting times, she knew that they were achieving much together. But what were they losing? Her awareness, and a profound one it was all her life, of the deep recesses of the individual in which the core of being existed made her say, again and again, that when Ruthie and Teddy married, four people were involved, not two. This was predicated upon her belief in "the divine androgyne," for she recognized not only the childhood tomboy in herself but also the male drive toward command and creativity. In her virile, commanding husband, she also recognized the sensitivity and the creative need of the female. Two people, but four beings, had been wed. And for the rest of her life, she sought to evade it, return to it, develop because of it, rediscover herself without it, and never quite relinquish it.

Buzz was in and out of the picture; Mother, comfortably settled in her own apartment, was there when needed; Father Dennis visited the new school from time to time; and Denishawn began to flower even as the great maverick herself began to wonder if her submission to a man who was "no weakling" had been wise. She never did find out.

Billing—that is, whose name came where—started right here, and it remained a critical item in the marriage from start to finish. St. Denis's name had star billing, then the company, and finally Shawn's name. He maintained that she had hired a partner and then was unwilling to give credit to the man himself. She, in turn, knew that she had world-wide fame and felt that he should earn equal billing. He was responsible for at least half the choreography and he assumed most of the responsibilities for running both school and company. Yet St. Denis was adamant, and the argument sputtered or raged, off and on, for years to come.

At the end of the first summer season of the school, St. Denis, with Shawn and their company, started out on a tour that would last almost eight months. Part of it was what they always called a concert tour, that is, they performed full programs of their own making in legitimate theaters from coast to coast. About half the tour represented vaudeville bookings and these they accepted, as St. Denis had done earlier, in order to make money, for before movies got big, vaudeville was the popular form of entertainment.

The tour of 1915–16, saw the addition of a major new work to St. Denis's personal repertory. It was a dance that was enormously successful in both concert and vaudeville, and it was called *The Spirit of the Sea*. St. Denis, famous for her manipulation of materials—saris, voluminous nautch skirts, peacock trains, etc.—here went further than she ever had before. The material in her own costume covered the entire stage! From her shoulders streamed yard upon yard of green silk in every direction. Her unbound white hair suggested the foam of the sea. The dance itself not only focused upon a virtuosic and unequaled manipulating of vast amounts of drapery but it also served notice that St. Denis, who had set all of her major creations within the framework of a specific culture—*Scherzo Waltz* and the *Impromptu* were considered as divertissements—could use her art to project images of elemental timelessness.

Although visually fascinating in its surge of silks, *Spirit of the Sea* was far more than a trick of staging. In late years, Miss Ruth would explain to a whole new generation of dancers and theatergoers that although some moments in her dances might justly be described as "Ruthie attitudinizing," her whole concept of the use of draperies and properties was firmly based in a belief that, for the dancer, draperies represented "an extension of the movements of the body itself into space." This she demonstrated in dance laboratory sessions which I conducted in the late 1950's by showing how weight, color, and even texture of the materials she used were selected in accord not only with the place and period of a given dance but with the movement itself. No one, not even Loie Fuller, exploited materials with such esthetic perceptivity. In her much later *Color Study of the Madonna,* St. Denis's use of color, weight, and texture in fabrics constituted a major choreographic element in the dance itself. In another dance, *Salome,* she did not simply strip off seven veils as the scenario suggested. She did not strip at all, but she *did* have seven veils, each totally different from the other and each representing a different mood or quality of action in the enchantress, for one was veiled seductively, another slithered like a serpent, still another suggested wantonness, and so it went. *The Spirit of the Sea* was the choreo-geographic peak of her relating of the movement of the body with the motion of her costumes.

In a somewhat later version, *The Spirt of the Sea* became a duet, with Shawn as a fisherman, lured by an unseen lorelei and drowned by the sea itself. There was something of an off-stage truth in this, for the young artist had always to fight submersion by a willful woman, a great artist, who happened to be his wife.

There is a tale, perhaps unfounded but very possible, that has to do with St. Denis's concern with both draperies and lights as they affected a later dance, *The Lamp*. It goes that at a stadium performance she had certain members of her company planted at strategic areas *under* the extended draperies whereby they could, lying prone, by specific movements, give the scarves an eddy, a ripple. St. Denis, fanatic about her lighting effects, was in a rage at this performance, for the lights were pink. Under her breath she muttered to one of the concealed sea urchins—and she was given to muttering and talking on stage—"Where's Anna?" The reply was that Anna Austin, a dancer who became an important St. Denis-Shawn soloist, was at the far end of the stage. "Send for her," was the command. The word was sent under the drapes and a body was known to be crawling its way up to the angry star. "What is it, Miss Ruth?" the voice queried. "Some idiot," said the star, "has used pink gels on me. I want my blue. Tell him." Off Anna squiggled her way and gave the order. The lights were changed. Anna crawled back under the yards of cloth to the feet of the boss. "Okay now?" she asked. "No," came the answer. "Wrong shade of blue." Apocryphal or not, it's typical.

On the 1915–16 tour, the company engaged a pickup conductor-pianist as a two-week fill-in. He remained for more than a decade. His name was Louis Horst. He became musical director for the Denishawns, composed for them, played for them, and when he finally departed, he joined an ex-Denishawn dancer and became her tutor, her guide, her composer, the most potent force in her career and, very probably, in her life. For she too was destined to make the greatest impact on American dance art in the generation to come. Her name was Martha Graham, and she came to the Denishawn School in Los Angeles as a student in 1916.

Young Martha, of Puritan descent, was shy and, some recall, a little awkward. St. Denis remembered that she herself taught her very little in the actual classes and that most of her technical training came from Shawn. But she knew her as an attentive, intense child who listened and watched and absorbed. Graham, when she herself had become a major star of the theater of dance, said, "Miss Ruth opened a door, and I saw into life."

The programs for the 1915–16 tour were as eclectic as the managers could hope for. There were St. Denis's famous Oriental dances and her gay *Scherzo* plus the new *Spirit of the Sea;* there were lusty, virile dances by Ted Shawn; there were romantic duets for the two principals; and there were dances that had to do with sports, the hula, and the most popular ballroom dances of the day and yesterday.

Their biggest and most ambitious undertaking to date came after the tour when they presented *A Dance Pag-*

eant of Egypt, Greece, and India at the Greek Theater
built by William Randolph Hearst at the University of
California in Berkeley. The pageant itself included
dances originally used in *Egypta,* revised for the new
production: Greek dances at which Shawn excelled, and
the East Indian dances in which both shared a common
interest. It was in this pageant that Shawn introduced an
all-male dance, probably the first created in the Western
world's cultures since the days of ancient Greece. The
whole pageant was then moved to Southern California
for presentations and then was adapted and abridged for
a long, long vaudeville tour. This was the start of the
Egyptian Ballet, rooted in *Egypta,* which, under vari-
ously related titles, was given more than three thousand
times by the Denishawns.

It was a grueling life, and St. Denis hated two-a-day
vaudeville, but she had accepted its monetary rewards in
the past and she would for the next few years, although
under protest.

The school flourished in its second summer, 1916, and
Shawn determined to make it a year-round enterprise
despite the touring commitments of the principals. He
engaged a faculty to teach, manage, and continue the
school curriculum, and this established a blueprint for
a workable plan to have authorized Denishawn schools,
in the years ahead, across the country. It meant that in a
given city dancers trained at Denishawn or by Ruth St.
Denis and Ted Shawn, could use the word "Denishawn"
in their promotion. The curriculum, of course, had to be
approved by the mother institution, and the stars them-

selves, in almost every case, agreed to teach locally each year for a given period of time. In Boston, for example, the famous Braggiotti sisters, of that remarkable family of artists known for their talents and great physical beauty, headed the local Denishawn school. They used Denishawn methods and taught Denishawn dances, and every year, one or the other of the Denishawn heads would come to inspect the school, note progress, introduce new advances and teach.

Indeed, 1916 was the first of a series of banner years for the Denishawns. St. Denis, the senior, although she disliked institutions, liked the position of passing on her dance knowledge and experiences to a generation of youngsters, of dance hopefuls. To them, quite naturally, she became "Miss Ruth," a term embodying both respect and affection.

In personal matters, the marriage had survived the first tests of ego, temperaments, conflicts in opinion, and those clashes born of work, weariness, professional jealousy (for they were on-stage rivals as well as partners), and too constant proximity. Indeed, after they had been separated for many years, Shawn reflected that it was an unnatural situation in which they lived. He pointed out that the average wife stays home with the children and has a life of housework or charities or hobbies on her own or with other women, while the husband is off at work for the day. At evening, they exchange news of the day and are grateful to be together. With the Shawns, the end of a day was a continuation of the work they had been doing together all day. There was no chance to say

"Dear, guess what *I* did today?" or "How are things at the office?" They knew what each other did and thought the clock around.

Still, with such problems there remained their intellectual and spiritual closeness with each other, their joint enthusiasm for Denishawn and its company and school, and the stimulation which their shared thoughts gave to the birth of new dances. And the love affair was still strong.

On the occasion of their second wedding anniversary, Ruthie wrote a prose-poem to her husband. It was lost and forgotten by both from 1916 to 1969 when Ted Shawn came upon an old wallet, unused, unseen, and packed away for more than half a century. In it, he rediscovered this intimate poem which he has most graciously granted me permission to reprint here. It is dated: "The little bungalow, 12th August, 1916." And it says:

Beloved!
        Two years!
So many great things have come to me
through you——my most inner soul
has come forth in new courage and
power because of you, and I am
so grateful! I did hope so much
from you—my eternal lover——
and you have not disappointed me.
    God knew, and we know
and this is only the beginning

Miss Ruth

I love you *with my Spirit*
my own—as well as with my
'pink and tender heart'
and with great faith, besides this
     millions of kisses
                    Thy own
                         R.

But after the long 1916–17 tour of the condensed
pageant program, the enlargement of Denishawn, and
the creative surging of both, World War I interfered
with two lives, with lives on stage and the personal lives
of two lovers. As many another before him and after
him, Ted Shawn enlisted in the United States Army in
order to serve his country. Ruth St. Denis was again
alone.

CHAPTER IX

To understand Miss Ruth in either 1917 or 1967, and all the years before and in between, it is absolutely essential to *accept* the paradoxes which made her what she was. To *excuse* her, no matter how generous the intent, would be to misunderstand her completely. She *did* worship the three gods—the Heavenly Father, art, love—and she was unfaithful. At one and the same time, if not in the instant at least in quick sequence, she was both worshipful and disloyal. She was spiritual and carnal— von Hofmannsthal recognized that in his brilliant analysis of her art.

She was reverent and irreverent in a matter of seconds, and this paradox should never have been subject to condescending forgiveness, for one was as much a part of her nature as the other. The androgyne—the recognition of the male element and the female element in all beings, and especially in all artists—was echoed in many other manifestations, in kindness and in cruelty, in arrogance and humility, in virtue and in wantonness, in discipline and in disorder. The biography of Ruth St. Denis, then, cannot be wholly a chronicle or a chronology, for the recurring constants in her life were her inconsistencies. Perhaps they were what made her a genius. Certainly, most great artists are, in essence, only normal people exaggerated into something more than the average person. So-called good points, or perceptivities, are exaggerated; so too are the bad points. Martha Graham has said that a temple without demons to warn as well as gods to guide us is no temple. Ruth St. Denis was proof of this. She too, from time to time, was aware of this.

In her eighties she was posing for her favored photographer of many years, Marcus Blechman, who captured her beauty and her magic in a magnificent history of her on film. Suddenly, she turned to him and said, "Marcus, I'm a very old lady. Soon I shall face my Maker. I've climbed, to use a cliché, the ladder of success higher than any American dancer except Isadora. And now, I look back in horror and realize that the rungs of that ladder were people." Mr. Blechman, telling me this story, said that for a moment he was terrified, for he thought that Miss Ruth had made her last confession, that Extreme Unction, or its equivalent, was in order, and that she was about to die. He was relieved when, a few moments later, she was "a bitch" again, and he knew that she would live.

He had been through it before and he knew her nature. He not only photographed her but he also designed make-up for her, and some years before, she had summoned him to help her with make-up for a performance in New York. He was happy to oblige, but when he got to the studio theater, she ordered him to go out for this and that as if he were a mere busboy. He did not protest; he simply said, "Miss Ruth, I photograph you and I make you up but I'm *not* your flunkey." Was she angry? Not a bit of it. "Fine," she said, "as long as it is all clear." So she found a flunkey. She found them all her life, for she needed people to wait on her, and she rewarded them with kind words or, perhaps, let them be a part of her theater. If you were weak enough to accede to her demands, she would use you; if not she *accepted* (not necessarily *respected*) a fact. She surrounded herself with some of the great minds but also with very usable menials. She needed both.

When I first got to know her, she assumed that I would print, in my newspaper, whatever she gave me. She learned I would not, unless I thought the news or pronouncement to be valid. Later, she would ask, write, or telephone and say, "If it's ethical, would you, etc. . . . ."

Somewhere, about 1957, she appeared on, talked on, and danced on a television show conducted by one of the most brilliant ladies of TV and radio, Arlene Francis. Out of the blue, Miss Francis asked her famous guest, if she could have a great dinner party whom, living or dead, would she invite. Quickly she named Mary Baker Eddy, the Empress Theodora ("She was a dancer, dear"), Will Rogers, and some others. Then Miss Francis asked what in heaven's name she would feed such a disparate group. Quickly, Miss Ruth suggested some kind of curry for the Empress, since she came from the Orient, and then went on to say that she would select corned beef and cabbage for Mrs. Eddy, because she "could do with a little matter." Now this was Ruth St. Denis, Christian Scientist.

In 1917 Ruth St. Denis, Christian Scientist, wrote in her journals, while curing herself of a dreadful cold and infection—she even called in a Christian Science practitioner—that she was battling "a mountain of error," all of which was good Christian Science creed, and then went on to say, "a battle is going on over the claim that I must have a pain in my rectum!"

In 1963 she was booked to go on a national tour with a show I had planned called *America Dances*. She had narrated it, and danced *The Incense* on it earlier at the Boston Arts Festival, but she came down with the flu and ultimately pneumonia, as we were about to take to the road. She tried, but she just could not make it. We set out and reported to audiences that the First Lady of the American Dance would soon join us. She could not. She called in that master of therapeutic exercise, Joseph Pilates, almost Miss Ruth's age, and a vigorous athlete at eighty, and although he exercised her, massaged her, and made her sweat, she got worse. Martha Graham, deeply concerned, late one night borrowed one hundred

dollars from a nearby liquor store and had Miss Ruth
hospitalized. Miss Ruth, being of age, disengaged herself
from the hospital and walked, either in sandals or
barefoot, in the snow, for some twenty blocks back to
her hotel.

Pneumonia was, of course, inescapable. I telephoned
her from the road—since I was pinch-hitting as narrator
for her—and I said bluntly, "Miss Ruth, you and I have
different views on healing. I can't use you as an invalid
or even as a convalescent, so get a doctor and I hope
that he's young and handsome." A few days later, in a
return message, she said that she was much improved,
that her doctor was young and handsome and that she
was "still, at my age, susceptible." She never made the
tour, but she was well enough to perform with *America
Dances* at the Harkness Festival in Central Park in the
summer of 1963. By midafternoon, thousands were lined
up across the park to see her dance, and when she closed
the show with *The Incense,* the thousands stood and
cheered. Her doctor was in the wings ready to give her
an injection for a possible repetition of the heart attack
which had followed her persistent refusal to have medication for pneumonia. But she did not need emergency
medication. Her tears fell to the stage with audible plops
as the audience paid tribute to her. Then, shutting off
the fountain, she turned to her adored dresser, costume-
controller of many years, Adolphine Rott, and chirped,
"Now that's over, let's go to Schrafft's and get an ice-
cream soda." And she did.

Her uncontrollable bursts of gay irreverence popped

out anywhere at any time, sometimes even in church. Once, long after Denishawn had come to an end and she was devoting herself to the building of her Rhythmic Choir and to the creating of religious dances on Christian themes, she staged a beautiful pageant of the Resurrection at a church in New York City. With great ingenuity taking the place of theatrical facilities, she devised a black ramp placed against a complex of black drapes. The Christ-figure, in white, moved backward up the ramp—she coached him carefully so that there was no sense of taking steps. You could not see the ramp since its blackness fused with the blackness of the curtains, and one saw what seemed to be a rising heavenward. A few weeks later, when someone asked her what happened to the handsome man who danced Christ with such beauty and dignity, Miss Ruth said, "Oh, Nicky has gone on to bigger and better things. He's now at Radio City Music Hall!"

But on the day itself when her staging of *The Resurrection,* in which she played Mary sorrowing at the tomb of her Son, was witnessed by a huge and deeply impressed congregation, she came to the pulpit, after the pageant was over, and delivered a sermon-address. She was dressed all in white, with the great Italian-wrought silver belt, her "Denishawn" belt, which her husband had had made for her, pulled tight around her still slender waist. Her snow-white hair, coiffed in what might be described as page-boy style, framed her face.

She spoke on religion and the arts and noted that, as in the Renaissance, both reached peaks of power and glory when they were wedded. She called for a renewal of the arts in the service of religion, and for religion to recognize the arts, including dance, as its voice. Then she spoke about love. Her accent was, of course, on Divine Love, and she stressed that in modern times we had cheapened the meaning of love. She referred to love affairs as reported in movie magazines and in gossip columns as contrasts to the deep love of which the spirit was capable. But she was not Puritan about it. "All I ask," she said, "is that you recognize *all* kinds of love." Then with that flash of the eyes which predicted a St. Denis irreverence, she suddenly blurted out, "And boy! do I know about all kinds!"

To the humorless ones, such a remark seemed to be a totally irreverent jolt, almost a negation of what she had said before. Because of it and other incidents like it, the formal church found her Christian dance projects possibly suspect. When I went backstage (or back-altar) to see her after this sermon, she said to me, "I ruined everything by that wisecrack. I know it, but it popped into my mind and popped out and I couldn't help it."

I told her that she was "half-mystic and half-mick" and she hooted with laughter. She made it clear that she was of English, not Irish, descent, but added that she sometimes behaved like "shanty Irish, not lace-curtains Irish, dear."

The outer biography of Ruth St. Denis has to do with the chronology of tours, of performances at home and abroad, of classes, interviews, rehearsals, comings-and-goings, but the inner biography is about an incredible being who was utterly and profoundly sincere in her desire to serve God through dance but who energized and humanized that service though an irrepressible and unpredictable bawdy wit, also God-given.

Even in her late years, when she was revered by the whole world of theater, sponsorship of some of her religious dance projects was not accepted by formal church organizations. She was, in certain instances, suspect, not because of morals but because of humor. She once said to me, "Dear, I have been called a prophet, and I think I am, but I shall always be a *minor* prophet because *major* prophets don't have a sense of humor."

But the ribald went right along, in wild conjunction, with the spiritual, the sensitive, and the profound. On that very tour, in 1917, when Ted was in the army and she was raising money for war bonds, she not only had her problems with healing, with Mrs. Eddy and the state of her rectum, she saw, recognized, marveled at certain wonders that led to a whole new area of her art. She was doing four shows a day on the Pantages vaudeville circuit. "I still remember it," she told me in 1967, "and it is all mixed up and yet a part of the whole. I saw Isadora dance a symphony. The next thing I remember is being in Edmonton, Canada, and seeing the miracle of the Northern Lights. I was in a restaurant, with treadmill service, and I seemed to see again Isadora coming forward with her unbelievable gestures. I went back to my hotel room. I thought how she reacted to the symphony—she didn't dance to it, she reacted to it. She went, it seemed to me, from marvelous gestures to wandering about until she was caught up again in the music. It was unforgettable, what she did, but it started me thinking, and somewhere, alone in Canada, I came up with the idea of a 'synchoric orchestra.' " The concept of this synchoric orchestra, which Shawn eventually carried to a peak of perfection in Mozart's *Symphony in G Minor* for himself and his men dancers, called for dancers to represent in movement the specific musical line of specific musical instruments. Thus, there would be a dancer who moved only to the passages of the first violin; another, to a wind instrument, etc.

Miss Ruth worked, pondered, created, laughed, misbehaved, worshipped, and rued wherever she was. Her portrait as a being consists of all these elements working both in conjunction and in conflict, on a high spiritual plane and on a purely physical one. To portray her in any other way would be to miss the forces which made her a genius, a personality, a star, and one of the most fabulous women the twentieth century has ever known.

The tours of Ruth St. Denis and Ted Shawn, separately (for they worked on their own from time to time) and together, combined triumphs with drudgery. This did not mean that they ever lowered their artistic standards, but it did mean that long cross-country tours seemed endless. Often they were not even quite sure where they were—that was the job of the company manager to get them, and the company, from the theater to a train and, at the next destination, guide them to their hotel. One morning they awoke and decided to go shopping. They had reached the city late the night before after a hop from another town. As they reached the street, Miss Ruth said, "Where are we, dear?" And Ted replied, "I don't really know, Ruthie, it looks like any average Middle West city. Anyhow, I have the route list with me, so we can look it up right now. What's the date?" Miss Ruth did not know the date nor did Shawn, and they had to go up to a policeman and, hoping they would not be arrested as vagrants, asked quite honestly, "Where are we?"

There is a story that following the smashing successes of their two-year tour of the Orient (1925–26) they made a triumphant United States tour and that in one city Miss Ruth was so carried away by the ovations from the audience that she gave a curtain speech in which she said, in effect, "We have danced all over the world, we have performed for maharajas and princes, but we are home at last and there is no audience in the world like you dear people of Detroit." It turned out that they were in Duluth, and the legend goes that when this was pointed out to Miss Ruth she said, "Well, they both begin with 'D,' don't they?"

CHAPTER X

THE chronology of life and of performing, however, went on. There was a St. Denis tour while Shawn was in the service of the military. There was a hiatus in the early 1920's when the Denishawn School became the Ted Shawn School while St. Denis set out with a company of girls, The Ruth St. Denis Concert Dancers. The reunion came and major national tours were renewed to be followed by the historic tour of the Orient. There followed the financially remunerative tour with the *Ziegfeld Follies,* the building of the ideal capital for American dance, Denishawn House, in New York City; the slow disintegration of a marriage, and the facing, for St. Denis, of a life and a career as she reached late middle age.

The years, as marked on a calendar, meant little. A schoolgirl in 1909 saw Ruth St. Denis in Boston, following her European triumphs. Fifty years later, she remembered the magic. But pick any year. Pick, just out of the hat, the year 1922, eight years after the marriage, seven years after the founding of Denishawn, three years before the fabled tour of the Orient, six years before the marriage foundered, nine years before the final bows of Denishawn. An average Denishawn year, 1922. What did America see?

Newspaper headlines across the nation reflected a vast change in the response of the press since the old days of 1906. Some 1922 headlines proclaimed: "RUTH ST. DENIS CAPTIVATES BIG AUDIENCE WITH DANCES;" "ACCLAIM ST. DENIS AND SHAWN DANCES;" "RUTH ST. DENIS DANCE THRILLS;" "RUTH ST. DENIS, TED SHAWN AND DENISHAWN DANCERS GIVE SUPERB ENTERTAINMENT." And so it went. The reviews themselves were filled with colorful descriptions of the art of Denishawn and a new understanding of the new stature of dance in America.

Robert Garland, in the *Baltimore American,* wrote at length about the performance he attended. He reported that "For two hours she held the audience spellbound," and then went on to say, "The catalogues call dancing the seventh art. Obviously it should be the first, as Louis Untermeyer has somewhere pointed out. It came before song, before speech. The childhood of the race was filled with dancing. Dancing was its sublimation, its apotheosis of fear, joy, anger, reverence, hatred, worship. And thus it is with Miss St. Denis and Mr. Shawn. The dance is their religion and their ecstasy.

"Last night they danced as we have never seen them

dance before; danced with body, soul and brain." And in taking special note of the *Egyptian Interlude,* he exclaimed: "First as 'Tillers of the Soil,' then in the 'Dance of Rebirth,' Miss St. Denis and Mr. Shawn displayed the full glory of the dancer's art. Here were brilliance, subtlety and physical beauty welded into one harmonious whole. Here were rapture, revelation and the ecstasy of movement. Here was something spiritual, but real, something to cling to and remember."

In Pittsburgh, the reporter, praising the entire program, stated that "In the *Brahms Waltz,* Miss St. Denis had the house breathless. It was one of the many glories of the evening." In Chicago, the reviewer ended his rhapsodic report with, "I consider the message of the Denishawns more direct than music, for it raises the human body to express the spiritual, individuality, purity and tells us the story of eternal art, much as could the trees and brooks if we but took the time required and really see them."

It would be wrong to assume that the spiritual manifestations of Denishawn dance were all that the reporters noted. The reason I have given it accent here is that it mirrored an entirely new understanding not only of St. Denis and her long-held goals, in 1922 almost a quarter of a century old, but of dance itself. For this, in America, was an accomplishment in a society which had long looked upon dance as wholly trivial and, at best, decorative. Decorativeness, however, in its proper place was an important part of the theater of Ruth St. Denis and, later, of St. Denis and Shawn. One bank of headlines stated: "RUTH ST. DENIS ENCHANTING IN WEIRD, EXOTIC DANCES, Colorful Settings Add Splendor to Production."

In the enormously popular *Spanish Suite,* Shawn won plaudits for his "Tango" (later, of course, he was to be cheered for his flamenco dances), while St. Denis was adored in "Shawl Plastique," in which the reviewers exclaimed over the beauty of the shawl itself and the movements of the dancer. In much later years, Miss Ruth would laugh and say, "Teddy was the Spanish dancer in the family. I had difficulty mastering heel-beats—I know now, from Mme La Meri, that I should call them 'taconeo.' But since about all I could do was a 'taconeo uno!' it seemed wise to make much of the shawl, which I did with the known St. Denis skill of manipulating materials, dear!"

Milwaukee, for example, babbled happily that "Probably the program offered by this famous ensemble was the most unique ever seen here, featuring, as it did, interpretations from many countries not usually sought out by masters of the ballet. Miss St. Denis and her husband have been widely heralded all over the world for the originality and gorgeousness of their presentations, a reputation which proved to be without exaggeration."

Miss St. Denis was the undisputed star of the troupe, with Shawn her closest rival—a situation which was the key conflict in their marriage. There were such praises for Shawn as ". . . *Thunderbird,* superbly done by Mr. Shawn in a costume which was as correctly magnificent as it was brief, and which set off his perfect figure to the greatest advantage . . ." plus "Mr. Shawn, as he danced the *"Tango,"* would have brought tears of envy to the eyes of Rudolph Valentino could he have been present to see. . . ."

Praises were heaped not only upon the stars but upon Louis Horst, the musical director, and upon such up-and-coming dancers as Martha Graham and Charles Weidman. The press, in Wilmington, Delaware, found that Miss Graham "has lots of personality and dramatic instinct as well as mastery of technique."

But always the praises focused on St. Denis. In Kalamazoo: "We have other interpreters of the dance—Pavlova, Genée, Duncan—but none of these ladies is quite equal to the versatility displayed by St. Denis and in none of their own special numbers are they stronger than she. . . . Sublime would be the word to describe it. . . . Kalamazoo vied with the effete East in its reception of the star and her associates."

The 1922 tour was the first of a series of the most successful tours by St. Denis, Shawn, and Denishawn. The 1919–21 hiatus, during which the stars went their separate ways theatrically except for special performances together, was at an end. There were three years—1922–25 —of extensive national touring under the management of Daniel Mayer, and it was during this period that Denishawn literally became a household word. By 1918 students from every state in the union and from foreign lands had come to the Denishawn School in Los Angeles to study a whole new way of dance. Starting in 1922, Denishawn was to go out to countless cities and towns in the States, and in 1925–26, to the world of the Orient.

Miss Ruth

Theodora, Greek Veil Plastique, and other important solos were added to St. Denis's personal repertory while she and Shawn were apart. During the Mayer years, she added one of her most ambitious productions to the Denishawn repertory. It was *Ishtar of the Seven Gates,* the ballet based on a Baylonian theme, and St. Denis's most elaborate production to date. Indeed, Shawn explained to her firmly that the very size of the production precluded use for touring—he once told me that "all seven gates opened and shut on hinges!"—so a modified staging was prepared for national trips.

In 1967, more than forty years later, Miss Ruth told me that she had visited Las Vegas, Nevada, with a highly commercial eye riveted on the acts used in the garish and rich gambling establishments, with their extravagant stage shows. *"Ishtar,* adapted," she mused, "would work. After all, she descends a flight of stairs slowly divesting herself of bits of array, while the hero is being tempted by her and a chorus of sensual females. Seems possible for La Vegas? disrobing? temptation? girls? Of course, I had a moral in *my Ishtar,* but we could eleminate that for Vegas!" She didn't live to do it. But she was willing, and what is more, Vegas was interested!

When the third triumphant Mayer tour came to a close in the spring of 1925, the stars and the company were engaged for summer appearances at Lewisohn Stadium in New York City, the first dance troupe to appear in this enormous, outdoor amphitheater. That they were a smash hit is clear, for they returned again and again to the Stadium, often featuring premières of lavish new productions. But the big news for Denishawn, and of momentous import for St. Denis, was the announcement of a tour of the Orient, the first ever given by American dancers, to run from the fall of 1925 for a year and a half.

Mayer had arranged for the tour of China, India, Japan, Java, and other Eastern lands with an Asian-based impresario, Asway Strok. During the long last part of the final Mayer American tour, St. Denis, Shawn, and the company did nothing while traveling by train but talk about the great adventure which lay ahead. They read books, they had talks by St. Denis and Shawn, questions and answers, preparations.

Oddly enough, St. Denis hesitated about going to the lands which, in fantasy and in study, had given her the food of her art. Was she concerned about taking her nonethnic creations to the cultures which had and could produce the ethnically, historically correct dances? The late Doris Humphrey recalled that Miss Ruth was nervous about this in advance but that when she was hailed as a great artist and inspiring prophet, all doubts disappeared. Or did she hesitate embarking on such a long trip because of the advanced age and frailty of Mother? Furthermore, she had long dreamed of going to the Orient but she had wanted to go by herself.

In her journals, she writes that after the three-year Mayer tour she had hoped for "rest and peace," but realized that "an objective period of harmony and solitude *will never come* unless I generate it myself—right where I am!" Her mercurial emotions are apparent here, for she wrote, "After all these years of loving a concept of Japan . . . and now? Just now I can find no thrill or enthusiasm about anything . . ." This was August 12. On August 15 she wrote, "I have come to gather the essences of these isles. I am as one returned home, a home of dreams from which I have been exiled."

Of the Tokyo opening, she said listlessly, "It went off mechanically as well as possible, considering the conditions . . . the audience was fair in size and fair in enthusiasm." The press was ecstatic and the Japanese public soon followed. The critics pointed out that the Denishawns had revealed that America was more than the "land of the radio and the automobile," and that it is "now creating its own art"; and that when historians come to write books about the relations between Japan and the United States, "they cannot ignore the coming of the Denishawn Dancers in 1925 to Japan." Another critic found the Denishawns to be working with principles "sympathetic to true Oriental souls."

This great rapport, through dance art, between Japanese and Americans, between Orientals and Occidentals, was echoed thirty years later when Martha Graham (who left Denishawn in 1923 and hence did not go on that tour of the East) took her own company to Japan and on her closing night was acclaimed through the bursts of hundreds of tiny firecrackers and tears at her departure; while in Indonesia, the press, saying that they had long supposed that America was a land of "money, gadgets and bombs," had discovered through Graham's art "that America has a soul."

A traveling repertory of several programs, with certain numbers interchangeable, proved popular everywhere. There were, of course, favorites which varied from land to land. St. Denis, in her autobiography, recalled that her *Ishtar* and Shawn's solo plastique of *Adonis*, in which his "marble-ized" body was clad only in a fig leaf, were popular everywhere. Doris Humphrey remembered that Miss Ruth's *Dance of the Black and Gold Sari* was "so popular and encored so often that you began to feel that every other number on the program was Miss Ruth in *Black and Gold!*"

Her journals note that en route to Shanghai she mused on the fact that she was "happiest, harmonious when dancing," and that "at Peking, at the Altar of Heaven, I saw my Theater of Heaven!"

In Singapore, she was taken with the idea of forming an Oriental group or society of dancers, with the dancers giving a short history "in talk and movement of the nation they represent." She characterized such presentations as "tale-talk" or "lecture-legend."

In Bombay, India, she records in her journal that she and Shawn had another discussion about giving him, after twelve years of partnership, equal billing. She quotes him as referring to his work with her as "twelve years of service." And with a charming understatement, she adds, "He is a rare and forceful personality." But she does not say that she acceded to his request, although she avers that "he is easily the greatest man dancer in the world today." At this time, they discussed warmly and enthusiastically the plan for a great studio, for the building of a Denishawn House on a lot they owned in New York's Van Cortlandt Park.

With considerable amusement, she writes about one of many experiences in India: "At the theater for three nights, we have danced before the Nizam of Hyderabad who is called the richest king in India. He and his wives and court are on the actual stage with us every evening. Last night, he gave me a book of his love poems in exchange for the bound volumes of our magazine [the *Denishawn Magazine*] which we had presented to him."

The whole occasion was "too grotesque and amusing . . . his clothes, his wives' clothes, and his manners, and his wives' voices yelling across from box to box— like ill-mannered servants on a holiday, the herding of them into the improvised purdah box on stage, etc."

In every place they played, they studied the native dances under the best dance masters available. They bought costumes and had costumes made. They made difficult and dangerous side trips to remote villages to learn more about the peoples of distant lands. Patiently, they sat through long epic dance dramas in Java, in India, in Japan. While performing on a grueling schedule and taking lessons continuously, they also spent hours in museums, temples, and in the company of the learned of many lands. And they never ceased to create. New works were begun, tested, even completed, and other vast projects were planned. There was enough material to serve Denishawn, the company of performers, and the schools with expanding curricula for years to come.

Throughout the long Oriental tour, St. Denis and

Shawn were treated with the same respect, honor, enthusiasm, and adulation that St. Denis had received in Germany and Austria twenty years before. Artists, philosophers, heads of state entertained them lavishly. Their influence was prodigious: in Japan, Japanese critics recommended that if Japanese theater was to be affected by the West, the Denishawns should be the model; in India, St. Denis's nonethnic Indian dances were credited with contributing to the renascence of India's classical dance; and China's greatest actor-dancer, Mei-lan Fang, was so impressed with the length of St. Denis's scarf, for she was a tall woman and he a short man, that he did away with no one knows how many hundreds of years of tradition and adopted the St. Denis scarf length, which immediately became the authorized one!

It seemed that Denishawn could go nowhere but up. In her journals, St. Denis reported colorfully—she was always a writer gifted with stunning imagery—what they saw and did and learned. But she also reported moments of loneliness, that strange inner loneliness and restlessness which was to plague her entire life ahead, as it had in the past. If there were sunny references to herself and her husband jumping out of the bed to share a view through a porthole on an historic journey, there were also those images in which she seemed to stand alone, uncertain, in desperate need of some kind of an inner peace which did not exist. In such moments, she rejected, even unwillingly, the person closest to her. While planning Denishawn House, a greater Denishawn, a dance theater and a revolutionary concept of education in the arts, she would jump, unpredictably, from enthusiasm to an inner rebellion against an organization which might trap the free spirit which she was always trying to find within herself.

On the long voyage home from the triumphant and enormously fruitful tour of the lands of her dreams, she wrestled with the directions she might pursue—with Ted, by herself, in loose tandem with Ted, free of institutional duties, serving the unprecedented dance plan they had made for America. As always she vacillated. Shawn later noted that she caused more havoc with her indecisions than with her decisions.

One final duty troubled her. She was weary of the three-year Mayer tour when she was persuaded to embark upon the great Oriental trip, and as they landed in America, she had behind her five years of intensive traveling. She wanted to dance more than anything else in the world, but "plans," "schedules," "organized projects" seemed to suffocate her. Still she knew that the Oriental triumphs must be exploited to the fullest, and so she accepted a United States tour under the famed Arthur Judson management.

With new productions, based on their Oriental studies, they headed east from California and dazzled a nation with the most elaborate costumes, settings, and productions that America, very probably, had ever seen. In the spring of 1927, they concluded the arduous tour with four performances in New York's Carnegie Hall. No one artist or attraction had ever performed four consecutive programs in Carnegie. Hundreds were turned away at each presentation. The cheers echoed through the famous temple of music. And such was the impact of the Denishawns that they were powerful enough to launch another new era in dance, dance criticism. They petitioned the New York newspapers, the *Times* and the *Herald Tribune* in particular, to engage dance critics. They pointed out that very minor musicians were given the courtesy of full reviews by competent critics, but that dancers were covered only by a few lines from a general reporter. The *Herald Tribune* was the first to respond by appointing as dance critic one of its music writers who knew a good deal about the dance art, Mary Watkins. A few weeks later, the *Times* appointed a young ex-actor, who was to become one of the world's most powerful and brilliant dance critics, to full-time dance duty. His name was John Martin.

The Denishawns were not only at the peak of American dance, they were very close to the summit of the world's theater dance.

And then Ruth St. Denis, unpredictable, did the unforgivable. At Carnegie Hall, with the bravos echoing and the audiences turning on adulations for the greatest American dance troupe, St. Denis, at one performance, chose to make a curtain speech. She thanked everyone for the enthusiastic reception and then went on to say that the response was such that she knew that *she* could fullfill a dream that *she* had long had, and that was the building of Denishawn House, greater Denishawn, the establishment of a dance theater. And she never mentioned Ted Shawn!

What she had fought *against,* she took for her *own,* and as the cheers rumbled, her husband, who had envisioned everything she was talking about, stood neglected in the wings.

At that moment, Ruth St. Denis heralded, unwittingly, the end of Denishawn, the end of a marriage.

CHAPTER XI

Before the swift decline set in, there were peaks to be scaled successfully by St. Denis and those around her. Brother, who had been prevailed upon by Shawn to stage manage the Oriental tour, not only danced occasionally in Oriental and American folk numbers but also used his free time to advantage by buying, and making arrangements for future acquisition of, Oriental materials. Shrewdly and tastefully selected, these purchases became the exotic stock of the St. Denis Asia Bazaar which he opened on Sunset Boulevard in Hollywood. He made the Judson tour following the return from the Orient, and then turned his full attention to the bazaar, which was to gain fame and earn money for years to come.

"It was successful," said Brother, looking back on it

in 1968, forty years after its establishment, "because it was a *practical* Oriental bazaar. The materials were not just decorative. They were made to be used in shirts, clothes of all sorts. And I had furniture too." The St. Denis Asia Bazaar had three different sites over the years, all on Sunset Boulevard, and the properties he owned became almost astronomical in value. There were successful branches in Palm Springs and Santa Barbara, so that Brother St. Denis, with his Wyoming oil continuing to flow and his bazaars enjoying great patronage, was by all standards a successful man, in business and in a happy home life with Em and the two sons.

St. Denis, too, on the surface, appeared to be rising to new heights of fame, accompanied by suitable financial rewards. The triumphant Oriental tour, the triumphant homecoming tour, added to the triumphant three-year pre-Orient Mayer tours of the United States and Canada, had made Ruth St. Denis and Ted Shawn the most famous theatrical artists, on a national basis, in America. Because of this, they were engaged as the stars of the touring company of the *Ziegfeld Follies,* since they were far better known to the country at large than were Ziegfeld's Broadway headliners. They took with them a unit of Denishawn dancers, but performed in "spots" separately from the regular Follies acts.

They did it, of course, for money. Denishawn House was under construction and it had to be paid for. The *Follies* was a dreadful chore—sometimes nine performances a week—and the tour lasted for thirty-eight weeks! The rewards, other than their popularity with audiences, were the dollars, an unbelievable three thousand five hundred per week. To earn well over one hundred thousand in a single tour, and with no manager's fee to pay, since the *Follies* management, not the Shawns, was responsible for the bookings, was a new financial feat for dancers.

They varied their offerings from time to time, but St. Denis's *Dance of the Red and Gold Sari* was a favorite, and oddly enough, considering the nature of a Follies-minded audience, so was Shawn's *Cosmic Dance of Shiva.* A new St. Denis solo, *A Legend of Pelée,* did not last very long. Shawn later recalled, "Ruth was always a mistress of multiple draperies, like in *Spirit of the Sea,* but this time she went too far and they mastered *her!* She tried to be not only the goddess of the Hawaiian volcano but the whole volcano too!" His description told of voluminous gray draperies which were the mountain sides, and that some kind of contraption around her shoulders was supposed to leave her arms free to dart forth with red scarves as erupting flames. She *had* gone too far, and the dance was dropped.

During a very brief respite in the Christmas holidays of 1927, Denishawn House was dedicated. Both stars spoke of the purpose of the new center, a personal home for them and a permanent home for dance in America. Then the irrepressible St. Denis placed a hand against the building, and instead of blessing it or pontificating further, wisecracked, "And every brick a one-night stand!"

The deadly routine, the commercialism of the *Follies*

tour only added to the inner St. Denis turmoils. She was now fifty years old and still unsure of her goals and her gods of Heaven, Art, Love. In Joplin, Missouri, she confided to her journals that she really wanted "to dance to soul music." In another town, she mused: "The old 'problems' of sex and love—of mating and morality! . . . Well, what *do* we believe—— As I have so often said, I really do not know!"

In some nameless town: "I am lazy."

In another, "Teddy said to me tonight, 'You need Mother'—I agreed."

In still another, "I hate practice and drudgery."

Since she was a star of national and international fame, an effort was made to have chic wardrobes selected for her and a fashion advisor to guide one who was meticulous in stage costuming and totally uninterested in street, or social, apparel. She was fully aware of this lack: "I know that I neglect my personal self in order to indulge my love for ideas and the impersonal. I've rather gloried in being the worst-dressed woman of the stage!" And she admitted to making up excuses "to justify my sloppiness."

Tensions between the two lovers, the two great dance stars, grew. They had always been man and wife on their tours, but now, in desperation, Shawn suggested a trial of separate, but nearby, rooms. But they could not stay apart for very long. The *Follies* was in Virginia: "Last night Teddy and I had a *deep* talk—old errors came to the surface. . . . He is so earnest and so boyish—and so naughty and full of ego, and the next moment, so humble and sincere—I love him so—but I must know that God loved him before I did. Perhaps after a period of being apart we can adjust our temperaments better than we do now."

A few days later, she wrote, "Said she of the lonely heart, 'I will create my own lover and my own God.'"

And as spring came in Canada, she said, "Yesterday, in the midst of my gloom, Teddy came into my room and said so sweetly and earnestly that he had been thinking about me—and really loving me—and wanted me to know that he stood solid and ready and at the center of things if I needed help! It was the voice of pure love talking and I was so grateful. . . . Love—it may be that in that subject I am still unsatisfied and adolescent."

As the seemingly endless tour went on, an emotionally uncertain Ruth St. Denis tried to analyze herself, in poetry and prose, in her journals. She was fêted everywhere, as was her husband, but alone she would write:

"I dance in the blue flame of sacrifice,

I dance the silent ecstasy of being."

And she would state: "The artist's nature is selfish—self-centered—drawing to him out of life only those elements that will feed the flame of his inner urge, his work."

Then, "I have talked and longed for love all these years, yet have never had the honesty, the courage to . . . love equally."

Her husband-lover and partner recognized this in her and tried his best to release the woman-wife from the stage-goddess. From her own inner torment, she wrote,

"I *must* go beyond the artist to the Saint. I must rise from imagination to realization of being."

Miss Ruth's journals, like Isadora Duncan's *My Life,* dwell but briefly on dance itself. Both are revelations of geniuses concerned not so much with their art, in matters of recording the years, but with their emotions. Only infrequently does she describe dances as such—a comment about Delsarte here, a remark about Japanese dance style there—for she deals mostly with dance concepts, both esthetic and religious, and on her own emotional experiences, passions, and doubts.

Of Denishawn she wrote, "It has existed because of the good and the true in our marriage."

Of herself, she wrote, "What self-centered, discordant personality these pages reveal!"

To me, she said many years later, "I was a very bad wife to a very good husband."

*   *   *

The very year of the rift, ironically, saw the creation of one of their most romantic and popular duets, *Josephine and Hippolyte,* choreographed by Shawn. He had given St. Denis a set of jewels that Napoleon had once presented to the Empress Josephine. These she wore as part of her costume in the duet that had young lovers and old lovers in their audiences sighing happily.

After the Orient, there were four more summer appearances at the Lewisohn Stadium, 1928, 1929, 1930, and 1931. St. Denis's first metaphysical ballet, *The Lamp,* to music of Liszt and with a huge cast, was given in 1928. In 1929, she danced with Shawn in his new Stadium work, *Jurgen,* based on the controversial James Branch Cabell novel and with a musical setting by Deems Taylor. In 1930, her special creation was *Angkor-Vat,* an elaborate ballet with a commissioned score by Sol Cohen. The fifth and final appearance of the Denishawns at the Stadium (1931) featured not only Shawn's *Job: A Masque for Dancing,* but also another mystical ballet by St. Denis, *The Prophetess,* and a music visualization, *Unfinished Symphony* (Schubert). This would mark the final time that the word "Denishawn" was to be used by a company headed by Ruth St. Denis and Ted Shawn. The posters, the headlines, the contracts read for the last time, "RUTH ST. DENIS, TED SHAWN and their DENISHAWN DANCERS." Shawn had been granted equal billing somewhat earlier, but Denishawn, as a union of two vital, creative spirits was vanishing.

Indeed, after the *Follies* tour, the two began to follow separate paths. There were tours together, even a tour as a duo, for commitments were always honored. But Shawn built himself a Japanese studio in Westport, Connecticut, and although St. Denis visited there, it was neither hers nor theirs. Shawn, in 1929, gave a sold-out solo recital at Carnegie Hall to rousing ovations. He toured, briefly, with some of the Denishawn dancers in the United States; and again as a soloist, he went several times to Europe for appearances which seemed to echo the success his wife had enjoyed a quarter of a century before. He too found Germany the responsive nation, and at one performance received forty-seven curtain calls.

St. Denis, however, was entering dark years. The Depression was on, bookings were difficult, and a scattering of performances, some of them back to the old society events appearances, were satisfying neither financially nor artistically. Shawn did not find domestic bookings easy without his famous wife's partnership, any more than she did without him. The team was gone, and money was hard to come by. He was better off, for he had organizational skill, a fine business sense and drive, and he was still young. She tried to run Denishawn House, valiantly, but she failed. There was no money left for mortgage payments. And so Denishawn, even as a school, disappeared. The house still stands, but it is no longer a home of dance.

The new Denishawn House had barely opened when decay set in. True, Shawn had engaged the great Swedish modern dancer, Ronny Johansson (who had danced with Denishawn in the *Follies*), to teach a new way in the ever-expanding pattern of dance exposure he had envisioned for Denishawn, and in his last year with the school itself, he had hired Margareta Wallmann, first assistant to Europe's modern-dance high priestess, Mary Wigman, to teach at Denishawn. She came, but it was too late. Martha Graham had long since left Denishawn, with Horst following her, to experiment with new ways of dance. As the Denishawn Dancers returned in triumph from the Orient with new exotica to attract an American public of unprecedented size for dance,

Graham made her first jarring impact on the American dance scene. She was not liked by many. She was ridiculed. Her sparseness and Spartan approach to the theater made her acceptable to a cult but also, as with Ruth St. Denis twenty years before, of interest to the intellectuals.

Doris Humphrey and Charles Weidman, left in charge of Denishawn while the stars were touring, were as restless as Graham. They experimented with new dance ideas by themselves and with Denishawn students. And before Denishawn had officially ended in 1931, they too had broken away to be participants in a whole new movement called "Modern Dance," a movement they shared wtih Graham, with Helen Tamiris, and later with a Wigman teacher and German expatriate, Hanya Holm.

Styles in dance were changing. The Depression had exiled luxury, and the new American dance reflected unrest, social injustice, ugliness. St. Denis had always fostered beauty. What was happening? The chicks who had fled the nest were dressing in what Graham was later to refer to, wryly, as "long woolens." Their themes had to do with revolt, hypocrisy, racial unrest, with strange abstractions like *Circular Descent* and *Pointed Ascent*, with barren boxes over which dancers crawled, instead of seven gates and golden stairs through which, and on which, gorgeously dressed (or undressed) dancers moved. St. Denis, the one-time revolutionary of the arts, could not understand the new rebels.

She and Shawn had literally forced the New York press to honor dance with the appointment of dance critics, yet John Martin, newly on dance duty with *The New York Times,* espoused the new dance movement and lit into the old guard. "Miss Ruth," Shawn recalls, "wept for days."

The dance rift was as bitter as the marital one. Graham, Humphrey, Weidman pulled away from St. Denis and Shawn; some of the things they said were worthy of new leaders, and others were reminiscent of children freeing themselves of their mother's apron strings. The terrible hurt was not healed for a decade. And then Miss Ruth, with her unquenchable spirit and judicious wit said, "I've been out of fashion for so long that when I got back in again, I didn't know it!" And she lived to see her "chicks" and their rebellious progeny return to the concept of dance theater which she originated and to the ideals of education in dance which Shawn, and to a degree herself, instituted.

But before the renewal were the long, bleak years. What she stood for was indeed out of fashion, and she herself had reached an age which, in youth-oriented America, made her seem old, yet an age which was not advanced enough to invite respect. Some years later, when Shawn was facing the same age doubts, she said to him, in effect, "When you're fifty, you're neither young nor old; you're just uninteresting. When you are sixty, and still dancing, you become something of a curiosity. And boy!, if you hit seventy and can still get a foot off the ground, you're phenomenal! So be patient."

With the end of Denishawn, with the dark years, with the estrangement of the married lovers for which both shared blame as their personal needs invited other, and conflicting, loyalties, came a vision of hope to an aging dancer. One night, awake, Miss Ruth had a dream of the Taj Mahal which she had visited not long before, and into her consciousness came a revelation which seemed to be the goal of her life. *Radha* had been a temple dance. She had danced the Japanese Kwannon and the Chinese Kwan Yin, goddesses of mercy, and she had weighed her own heart, and soul, against the feather of truth, in the ancient temple of Osiris in her *Egypta*. She knew, instantly, that the final cycle of her career would be the fulfillment of what the POSTER had breathed into her thirty years before. In her autobiography, she described it with lovely simplicity: "These dances would be done in a beautiful temple building, on an altar-stage, large enough to permit all manner of sacred ballets, in an auditorium with no pillars so that the line of vision would be perfect. Studios and classrooms would be above the auditorium, and galleries for the exhibition of graphic arts." The concluding sentence of this statement of purpose read: "At all times, I described it as a place which had the motivations of the church with the instrumentation of the stage." This indeed was Miss Ruth speaking.

From this vision sprang her Rhythmic Choir, her Society of Spiritual Arts, her Church of the Divine Dance, and innumerable other projects dedicated to a liturgy of dance for theater-church.

She never quite succeeded in doing what she set out to do. She *did* dance in great churches; she *did* enlist the enthusiastic aid of ministers, priests, rabbis, monks, Moslems, Buddhists in her unending project; and she exerted a tremendous influence on those Christians who wished, as did she, to restore dance to the service of the church. But there was never another *Radha,* another *Egypta,* another *O-mika.* There were such glorious dances as *Color Study of the Madonna,* the *Blue Madonna of St. Marks,* the *Gregorian Chants,* but the audiences were much, much smaller, and there was no question that the impact which *Radha* had caused in 1906 was *not* repeated in 1936, '46, '56, or '66. But she never lost faith in the final destiny of her art, for in 1968 she told me of her plans for a great, new dance, *Rhythms of the Resurrection.* She was old by then—ninety-one— but the ardor was as fierce as when she had broken with Belasco and security and convention to bring a new way of dance, of theater, of dancing spirit to the entire world.

CHAPTER XII

With the foreclosure on the mortgage of Denishawn House, the once great star had no place to go. Friends came to her rescue, as they always did, and gave her a place to live and to rehearse. It was tiny, after the spaciousness of Denishawn, but it was a home. For a while she moved in a dulled trance, not knowing where to go, what to do. She was, literally, passée.

After a time, she reassembled her Rhythmic Choir and began to hold meetings and give studio presentations of religious dances. Among those who attended faithfully were Dr. and Mrs. Paul Dawson Eddy. Some years later, and in due course, Dr. Eddy became president of Adelphi College and was able to give Miss Ruth a renewed career by inviting her to found, in 1938, the Dance Department at Adelphi College on Long Island.

She was wise enough to know that she couldn't really organize a college dance program, so she engaged a highly competent faculty, among its members Jack Cole, a St. Denis student, a major participant in Shawn's first all-male dance presentations, and a jazz dancer of uncommon skill and taste.

But before Adelphi, came the programs for Rhythmic Choir events, several masques and pageants for churches (some of them highly successful), an occasional vaudeville appearance (she danced at the old Paramount on Broadway), and some teaching. But she was sinking slowly into obscurity. Shawn had bought an old farm in the Berkshires and had made it his headquarters. His post-Denishawn tours with a company of men and women dancers had ended, and he, too, was literally broke. He secured a job teaching at Springfield College, a school of physical education, and from there went on to found, in 1933, what was to become the world-renowned company of Ted Shawn and His Men Dancers.

Miss Ruth, despite her activities in dancing for the church, had to wait until 1937 for her theatrical rebirth. The occasion was a vast festival, called Dance International, which was held at Rockefeller Center in New York City. Movies, still photographs, sculptures, paintings, lectures, demonstrations were seen over a period of two months, highlighted by performances in the huge Center Theater (now demolished), across from Radio City Music Hall, by American ballet companies and modern dance groups. Miss Ruth was invited to appear with the moderns as if in tacit agreement that she had something to do with the origins of not only some of the dancers (Graham, Humphrey, Weidman, and many others) but of modern dance itself. The transitional period of rejection, of antagonisms, of a generation gap was almost over.

It was for this occasion that I pinched pennies and borrowed money to journey from Boston, where I had my first dance critic's job, to see a legend. "Smitten," I think, was the word for my reaction, for although she was sixty years old then, she literally illumined the stage with her presence. Others in that vast audience were smitten also. In commenting on her comeback, she later said, "I guess a lot of them thought that Ruth St. Denis should be dead by this time, so when I came on stage, it must have been something of a surprise." Indeed, after her last Stadium performances with Shawn, she had slipped so far from view that a good many old-time dance fans assumed she had died (or, at the very least, retired) and the new dance followers, the teenagers, had never heard of her, unless they had read their history books.

Returning to the stage as a historic figure in dance solos which were themselves historic made her realize that she could quite effectively capitalize on her cele-brated past while continuing her dedicated work in the field of religious dance. Bored, for so long, with the old Oriental dances she had been forced to do endlessly on tour, she came back to them, after the long respite, with new affection.

She met, at this time, a remarkable woman whose

dance roots went deep into all forms of ethnic dance but most deeply into the dances of India. She too was an American and her name was La Meri. She was born Russell Meriwether Hughes, but in Texas, where she grew up, the Mexicans refused to call her Russell, because that was a boy's name, and they could not pronounce the last half of Meriwether, so they called the little girl who loved to dance, La Meri.

Like St. Denis, she started her theater life in vaudeville. She did toe numbers, Mexican dances, Spanish dances, and very often she danced with her older sister, Lilian. The Hughes girls were quite the talk of San Antonio. But they went on. They even played the vast Hippodrome in New York. La Meri wanted something more. She traveled around the world. She studied in every land she visited; she mastered alien tongues and alien gestures, and because of a God-given gift for instant absorption, she could identify not only her steps but her actual being with a variety of races.

She returned to America, after years abroad, as the world's greatest performing expert on ethnic dance. It was she who introduced the word "ethnologic" into the world's dance vocabulary, and it was she who knew and revered Miss Ruth's immeasurable contribution to the Oriental dance, in the Orient itself as well as in the Occident. The two joined forces in 1940 and formed the School of Natya in New York. Both taught, both danced, and although neither was given to enjoying the company of other women, they got along famously. They had their studio-theater at 66 Fifth Avenue, and La

Meri, at the last minute, prevented Miss Ruth from saw-
ing a priceless Javanese gamelan in half—"just so I can
have two instead of one, dear"—and cutting up an ir-
replaceable gold-thread sari for a rumba costume. (Miss
Ruth called everyone, including people she had just met,
"dear," for the simple reason that she was always uncertain whether she had met them before or not. Since
some were ex-escorts, who had been forgotten, this
seemed the gracious approach.)

She and La Meri worked well together, although La
Meri was thoroughly organized and Miss Ruth totally
disorganized. One of the results of their collaboration
was a joint recital in New York in which La Meri did
the "authentic" dance and Miss Ruth the "art deriva-
tive." So, for example, the audience saw a classical invocation in Bharata Natyam style juxtaposed with *The
Incense,* or a traditional peacock dance set side by side
with the St. Denis *Peacock.* The result? It was not a
contest but a partnership, and so neither had to win.

In 1941 Miss Ruth was settled in a big apartment on
East Fifty-ninth Street once occupied by Isadora Duncan, and the following year she and La Meri combined
the School of Natya with the Ethnologic Dance Center.
For St. Denis, the Oriental phase was back in full swing.
A high point of the comeback occurred on July 11, 1941,
when the great British ballet stars, Alicia Markova and
Anton Dolin, invited St. Denis to perform at Shawn's
Jacob's Pillow Dance Festival which they were directing
for that particular summer. They prevailed upon her
to dance the program which had launched her concert

career thirty-five years earlier at the Hudson Theater.

I remember watching a rehearsal in the old barn-studio at the Pillow—the Ted Shawn Dance Theater would not be built for another year—in company with Emily Coleman of *Newsweek*. Miss Coleman had never seen Miss Ruth before and knew of her only through dance books and her mother's memories of having seen Denishawn. At this rehearsal, Miss Ruth was at her sloppiest. She was wearing an elaborate *Radha* headdress, quite different from the original one, a brassiere and a greyish-pink girdle. She was "marking," as performers often do, that is, just outlining steps and patterns to the musical beats.

She looked old, a trifle bent, the flesh bulging over her girdle, the old Denishawn knees overlarge and somewhat knocked. Emily, I recall, nearly wept with sorrow for the old lady who seemed bent on destroying her own legend. "Wait," I hissed. Miss Ruth continued to mark until the particular variation neared the finish. The music raced up the scale, and she began a low, fast turn which spiraled upward and, on the last note of the music, culminated in a pose of breathtaking beauty as the body stretched upwards and the raised hands seemed to brush the sky. With understandable and excusable irreverence, Emily exclaimed, "JESUS!" The revival was a smash hit.

The historic occasion did not go unrecorded. John Martin, the dean of American dance critics, gave her a rave notice and reported that "it was one of the earliest works to treat the dance as a serious independent art capable of spiritual values," and he went on to say of

Miss Ruth in *Radha* that "her performance itself made clear her right to the title of the first lady of the American dance." I wrote of the event in the *New York Herald Tribune,* using an old photo with the famous swirling skirt and backbend taken in 1906 and a brand-new photo, taken by Dwight Godwin, shot in 1941.

The old photo, though simulating action, was not actually a true speed-action shot. With her marvelous inventiveness, St. Denis, in 1906, had invisible threads attached to the great gold skirt in *Radha* and had invisible humans, out of camera range, pull them taut as she went into, and held, a backbend. The result was a shot which looked as if she were spinning. In 1941, she did not really want to do the backbend for the still camera, but I was present at the photo session and insisted: "Miss Ruth, please try it, and if it turns out all wrong, we'll burn the negatives." With a very ungracious grumble, she agreed, and Godwin got an historic shot of her in action. She knew it the instant the shutter clicked, and suggested we do more!

Godwin was also at Jacob's Pillow and filmed *Radha,* in its entirety, as a movie. It was done out-of-doors in the blazing sun on a platform just outside the studio. But the fabulous St. Denis make-up and the beauty of the woman herself withstood the harsh lights, and the piece, though done under primitive filming conditions, did honor to a great artist. But only now is the Godwin *Radha* being edited, given a sound track, and provided with a prologue putting the work in historical perspective, according to Miss Ruth's own specifications, for release in 1970–71.

With ovations ringing in her ears, Miss Ruth went from the Pillow to other engagements, including four recitals at the Carnegie Chamber Music Hall. Local and international press took note: "Miss St. Denis carried her audience as completely as she ever had"; "Ruth St. Denis is an amazing woman—by all odds the most amazing dancer ever produced in this country and certainly the most colorful and interesting of women"; and, on tour, "Norwalk was honored last night with the appearance of one of the greatest dancers the world has ever known, Miss Ruth St. Denis."

She discovered the value of the "historic dances" and did them frequently. *Radha*, requiring a setting, props, and a cast did not continue for long, but *The Incense, The Cobras*, and other old solos remained in her repertory for another quarter century plus! This did not mean that she relinquished creativity. To the contrary, she was constantly at work on her Rhythmic Choir offerings; she took a crack at the rumba; she did some acting; and she appeared at Adelphi College in a really stunning work created by Jack Cole. This was in the late 1930's, and Jack, in a progress report in letter form, wrote me: "Miss Ruth is learning to count and look like a modern dancer." The piece itself was a remarkable concept of treating the New Testament as a primitive mystery. Miss Ruth was the Leader of the Chorus, and she both spoke and danced. I shall never forget her, wearing a floor-length crimson costume and with her snowy hair falling to her shoulders, striding upwards from one platform to another until she reached the apex, and throwing wide her arms, saying in her lovely voice, "My God, my God, why hast Thou forsaken me?"

Behind the scenes, not all had been serene. Cole, a devoted pupil of Miss Ruth, was known for being difficult, and at one rehearsal he had lost his temper and called her an old hag. She threw herself on the stage and screamed, Cole ran out of the college building and headed for the railroad station, with a chorus of distraught females, wearing classical Greek garments and stylized leather wigs, in hot pursuit, urging him to "Come back!" He later told me that the train pulled out just as he got to the station and since the timing was all wrong, he returned to Adelphi and peace was made.

Miss Ruth, in the early 1940's, danced frequently in the old Duncan studio on Fifty-ninth Street. She toured. She was back in business. In her sixties, as she had predicted, she was considered remarkable.

The return to the stage, the re-recognition of her dance stature gave her new courage and, of course, fed that insatiable ambition which was, until the very end, an inextricable part of her being. The ego, obviously, was perfectly secure—she knew, quite simply, that she was a genius, and she was not really concerned with possible rivalry with others, her husband excepted. But the ego needed to be fed—constantly. She was always surrounded by hangers-on, those who would do her bidding for a crumb, out of genuine devotion or in the hope that something would happen to them because of the association. Her lovers, and she had them, fed the ego as well as answering her sex desires.

In her autobiography she freely admits to her affairs, most of them rooted in romantic fantasies. In a remarkable letter, written in the summer of 1939, to her estranged husband, she makes confession. She had been caught up, as several times before, in the Oxford Movement (Moral Rearmament), and she was cleansing herself. By Ted Shawn's permission—he gave me, after Miss Ruth's death, a copy of a letter seen by no one but himself for thirty years—I can quote from this amazing confession of a woman who was virginal until her marriage in her thirties and then sought promiscuity. I do not present part of the contents of this letter for purposes of sensationalism—for what is sensational about sexual promiscuity these days?—but because they reveal an aspect of a great artist, a tormented woman.

"Dearest Ted, There are curious spiritual upheavals that go on in all of us I suppose, some of them subtly under the surface and we are scarcely aware of them, and others that are all too obvious in their suffering and consequent release.

"I am now thinking of my life all the way back and all the way forward [she had another twenty-nine years of life ahead of her]. It is all a great mystery. Should you and I have ever come together and married at all? . . .

"How the seeds of dishonesty, self-indulgence and self-pity were in *me* from the beginning. So shallow and insincere when I prided myself on being so honorable.

Selfish to the last degree when I had an illusion of being so generous. . . .

"All mixed up about you. Desiring you without ever being willing to pay the price. Married and yet not married. Stupid blind egotist! No wonder you couldn't live with me. No wonder your manhood was thwarted and distorted by my constant assumption of superiority. . . .

"Floored constantly by vanity, pride and sensuality, faintly underhand, cowardly. Attracting defenseless boys who need a friend and mother and instead find an impossible lover. A woman twice their age who does not know what to do with them once she 'gets' them. . . ."

"One who has been told that she gave 'beauty for ashes' but who now knows that much of the time she gave ashes for beauty, because she bartered her love for pride of place and power. . . .

"I am seeing you with new eyes. You not only have made an enormous contribution to the spiritual and art life of America and the world, but you will probably make a new and different one before long. . . . American youth is looking to you as never before, and you will not fail them. . . .

"I honestly don't *know* why I am sending this to you now. I seem impelled to, that is all. You are and you are not interested in my unfolding life, you have plenty of inner labors of your own. Yet I feel there is a value for us both that as far as I am capable, I am letting all bars down of resentment and criticism and deadness of feeling. This last is very vital because, Ted, when we do this we die . . . don't you think so? I mean that when we grow indifferent and dead to any human relationship, we are dying in our whole being . . . ever your Ruthie."

*　　*　　*

With the coming of World War II, Miss Ruth participated in benefits for British War Relief, Russian War Relief, and other Allied causes, and then hied herself to California where, for a time, she worked (as a riveter!) in the Douglas Aircraft plant. There were plenty of publicity stories about this, and I remember, as a soldier, flying the Atlantic from Africa back home, that a friend leaned over to me as we were mid-ocean and said, "I know you love her dearly, but I hope Miss Ruth didn't have anything to do with *this* plane."

While she was working patriotically in an aircraft plant, she was also pondering on war, on man's nature. She wrote innumerable poems on the subject. One that she sent to me included these lines:

These parts of machines
These assemblings
These earnest, intelligent, feverish workers
Putting their minds on the problem
Their hands to the task
These planners and changers
These gatherers of raw materials
These triumphant presenters of the finished plane
I say
What are you doing this for, my friend?
Do you know, and if you do not, do you inquire?

Or do you speak only of work and wages
And your rights?
To what does it all lead?
To five minutes or less
Demoniacal destruction
To falling metal
To falling bodies
To blasted cities
To silence and grey death.

It was during the war years that Miss Ruth moved to California and made it her home—although she traveled and toured extensively—for the rest of her life. Brother had built for her a lovely studio-home on Cahuenga Boulevard. On the ground floor there was an enormous studio not only large enough for classes but also for performances, plus other rooms, including a big kitchen. There were rooms on the second floor, a little garden in the back, a side yard large enough to use as "location" for filming, a fabulous view of her beloved mountains, and right next door, Brother and his family.

It was in the kitchen, however, that Miss Ruth elected to live. Since her possessions included everything from her gold Buddha and lavish costumes and settings to trunks of jewelry (mostly costume jewelry), books, scrapbooks, vast charts (she was always making charts of temples, pageants, and even governments!), thousands (maybe millions) of photographs, untold clippings and brochures she was always having printed, there was no "living" space for herself. She had her bed moved into the kitchen and surrounded it with orange crates filled with the projects of the moment and yesterday's forgotten projects. Brother installed bookcases for her in the kitchen, but these were soon filled and back came the orange crates. It was a mess, but then, wherever she lived took on the image suggested by that line from Herrick, "a gay disorder."

She could go into a hotel room, and in less than five minutes the bed would be piled with nautch skirts and books, the bulletin board would be up, the charts spread all over the floor, and the lady would be ready for business. Naturally, the shoes came off first (most dancers live barefoot at home), and she could plod easily over and among her cherished debris. Usually, she could find what she wanted, but if not, there was always someone there to receive the order, "Get that new chart, dear." When she would go out, she would sometimes, absentmindedly, forget her shoes, or the floppy gold sandals she used for streetwear in her last years. Once, after a rehearsal, she charged out onto the street in the pouring rain, hat on but no shoes, and as she hailed a cab, one of the dancers, in full Oriental make-up, tore after her calling, "Miss Ruth! Miss Ruth! You forgot your shoes!"

When she stayed with friends, instead of at a hotel, the picture was the same: disorder. Sometimes she would visit her beloved Adolphine, who dressed her, pressed her costumes, and sewed her up for many years. I telephoned Adolphine one day in order to track down Miss Ruth. Adolphine took a long time to answer the phone and I expressed the hope that I had not called while she was busy with lunch or costume repairs or something. "No," she said, "I was simply cowering in a corner. I guess I was trying to hide for a little while. After all, I'm an old lady of seventy and I just can't keep up with her." Miss Ruth, at that time, was in her mid-eighties.

The Cahuenga studio became not only a school, a theater, and storage space but also the headquarters for the Ruth St. Denis Foundation, which presided over her plans for a temple of the dance, her Church of the Divine Dance, the Ruth St. Denis Intimate Theater, her movie projects, an arts colony, and all the other blueprints which filled her constantly inquisitive mind.

In the 1940's and 1950's she was busy with her center in Hollywood. She thought about trying to establish her arts colony in New Jersey near the old farm; she investigated land in Connecticut for the same purpose; she purchased property in California for her arts colony and learned, to her great pride, the difference between "sinking" a well and "digging" one.

She and Shawn were no longer estranged. The brilliant period of Shawn and his men dancers had ended with World War II, when most of the boys went into military service. He turned his attention to Jacob's Pillow, which he had purchased as a comfortable farm retreat but which had become a dance center. After the revival of *Radha* at Jacob's Pillow, Miss Ruth came frequently to dance on the summer-time festivals. Sometimes they danced together again in *Tillers of the Soil* and *Josephine and Hippolyte*, not only at the Pillow but elsewhere, such as on the very popular "Around the

World With Dance and Song" series at New York's Museum of Natural History.

As they aged, they mellowed somewhat. Rivalry, mostly past rivalry, was still present, but Shawn was ever the cavalier, and when he introduced his "beloved wife" from the stage of Jacob's Pillow, there was still the echo of the Denver student who had had his life changed by a stage goddess. They held hands again. They went off to private dinners. They visited until the late hours of the night. What they said belongs to them.

She danced to cheers in the Philharmonic Auditorium in Los Angeles, and she danced at that unique dance center in New York, the Kaufmann Auditorium of the Ninety-second Street Y.M. and Y.W.H.A., which William Kolodney had built into one of America's most important dance laboratories. She danced at the Hollywood Bowl. She danced for me in lecture-demonstrations and television shows. She performed in Chicago, and a block party was held for her to overflow crowds. The tributes poured in. Cannily, she said, "They're paying tribute *this* year to me, and I'm grateful, but I can't expect it *next* year too. Ruthie has got to get to work."

Canniness, despite her wild disorder, was always a part of her. John Martin had asked her to appear on a big benefit at Carnegie Hall and she decided to do the *Dance of the Black and Gold Sari*. There were to be many other dance stars on the program. Then, he asked her if she would open. She had never opened a show, except a solo recital, for half a century. John called me, told me what he had planned, and explained that he wanted Miss Ruth to appear first as a sort of "mother of us all," and, he added, that the lady herself would probably call me and ask what I thought. She did. I explained and recommended. Then she said that she would change her solo to *White Jade*. The reason: "In *Black and Gold* I do turns, and I'll be followed by those ballet people who can turn longer and faster than I do. By the end of the program I'll be forgotten. But who else will pick up this, put it down, touch another thing, stand, look and gesture? No one but me. At the end of the program, *I* will be remembered over all the turners." She was quite right.

Very often, in her eighties, she would travel alone. Someone would get her onto a plane or train and someone else would meet her, but she had no second thoughts about journeying alone. Even in New York City, the streets held no terror for her. One night she asked me to take her to dinner. Where did she want to go? The Oyster Bar at Grand Central Station! She showed me the choreographic patterns of *Ishtar* with salt and pepper shakers, forks, spoons, bits of ripped-up rolls. Then she put her shoes back on, grabbed a case that had heavy records in it, clutched an Oriental shawl loaded with heaven knows what, and announced that she would like to tramp home alone, along Forty-second St., remembering when it was a street of theater and not junk movies, up to where she was staying in the West fifties. I hesitated about letting her go off by herself—she was in her seventies then—but when you were dismissed by Miss Ruth, that was it.

She was using an apartment belonging to William Skipper, dancer, choreographer, and a disciple-friend until her death. I called Billy a few hours later to be sure that Miss Ruth had reached home safely with all of her impedimenta. "Is she okay?" reiterated Bill. "She's dancing!" Skipper, in New York or Hollywood or anywhere, always remained close to her, and it was he who produced a color film, made in the 1950's, of four of her great solos (*The Cobras, The Yogi, The Dance of the Black and Gold Sari, White Jade*), directed and photographed by Marcus Blechman.

To make this movie, she worked hard and lost weight for the camera. The diet sapped her strength but she did look svelte. The results were lovely, but she herself said, "It should have been done five years ago."

Her energy had to do with naps. As a child on the New Jersey farm, her mother had given her Delsarte relaxations. She never forgot them. When she was tired, wherever she was, except on stage, she rested. In dressing rooms, she would spread out a big nautch skirt and cat-nap before a performance or even between numbers. She came to my house in the country and said to my mother, "Along with everyone else, you probably think I'm phenomenal. This is my secret," and she charged in the door, threw herself on the sofa and went instantly to sleep. Twenty minutes later, she ordered tea and then said, "Now I shall be a proper guest."

She told me once that being physically tired was good for you, but that being fatigued, in which nerves were involved, was bad. She avoided fatigue through naps.

The "More Living Life" of Ruth St. Denis

Toward the end of her life, she said, "Naps have always been important to me. Now that I am older, they are longer and more frequent, and someday, in God's good time, I shall take the last nap of all."

*   *   *

Miss Ruth never lost her interest in acting, and in her journals and letters she referred to the possibility of her turning into an actress again as she got too old—which she never did—to dance. When in her seventies, she took on the taxing leading role in Giraudoux's *The Madwoman of Chaillot* in a successful summer theater production. Some years later, at Jacob's Pillow, she was engaged in some dance poses for John Lindquist, the Pillow's official photographer and a long-time friend, when she blurted out, "John, enough of the dance things for a moment, I want you to catch me as Bernhardt," and she struck attitudes instantly reminiscent of photos of the great French actress.

Indeed, in 1919 her husband reported that the role she played in a drama especially written for her, *Miriam, Sister of Moses,* would have indeed challenged a Bernhardt. It was written for her by Constance Smedley, an old friend from her early dancing days in Europe, and Maxwell Armfield, and Shawn played Moses. St. Denis received excellent reviews hailing her acting skill, her voice, and her diction. It was presented in the Greek Theater, a gift to the University of California from William Randolph Hearst, and there is a plaque which so states. St. Denis had a line in the play which referred to "the heart's corruption," but instead, with a dramatic gesture, she proclaimed, "I shall make visible the *hearst* corruption!" No one ever knew whether it was a slip of the tongue or, knowing the St. Denis wit, intentional. She would never say.

As the years went by, she did other plays, among them Wilde's *Salome,* in which she danced as well as acted, and the popular play *The Royal Family.* Both of these were done for Daniel Reed and his wife, Isadora Bennett, in their summer theater in North Carolina. By this time Miss Ruth was having difficulty remembering her lines. Before going to Carolina she was at Jacob's Pillow and she asked Shawn's composer-pianist, Jess Meeker, if he would hold the book for her and correct her when she went off the speech. Naturally, he tried to give her the cues by reading the last line of the character speaking before her. After a few minutes she startled him with, "Enough of that, Jess. I'm going to have trouble enough learning my *own* lines without being bothered by what *other* people say." Meeker said later, "I think Miss Ruth learned the whole play as if it were an uninterrupted soliloquy."

And indeed she did have troubles. In doing *Salome,* she kept agreeing to Herod's request to dance much too soon, and in *The Royal Family,* Miss Bennett, who was holding the book, had strategic sites for herself. These included not only the customary prompter's box but also a trap door and a fireplace behind which she crouched. It was a nerve-shattering experience for Miss Bennett and, of course, for the cast. In one scene, when several people were on stage, Miss Ruth hissed to the actor next to her, "What's my next line?" Since she had gone so far afield by that time, the actor didn't know, so he whispered to the next actor, "What's Miss Ruth's next line?" The query traveled all the way to Miss Bennett who fed a line which, in turn, traveled back, in relay, until it was given to Miss Ruth. Blithely she said, "That won't do, dear. I've already said that one."

Oddly enough, it was not disaster, and no one in the audience knew that anything was amiss. I asked one of the actors what Miss Ruth was doing while waiting for her line, and he said, "I was too nervous to notice, but I think she did a western version of her Japanese Flower Arrangement!" Miss Bennett, recalling the occasion in 1969, said, "Oh, it looked fine. Dan did a great job of directing—he knew how to handle Ruth—and Ruth is such a performer that she couldn't miss. That the rest of us turned white-haired overnight, and were jibbering idiots by the time she left us, were simply private, tragic consequences to her performance."

On another occasion she worked with Dan Reed in New York. She was choreographing the dances for a Mother's Day pageant based on the biblical Sarah. For her finale, she had the cast cross the footlights and come down into the audience. One of the performers said, after several rehearsals, "Miss Ruth, after this do we go back on stage or up the aisles or what?" "I'll set it later," was all she said. At dress rehearsal, she still hadn't set anything to get the company out of what was admittedly a striking finale. So as she dismissed them, one voice said from the audience side of the footlights, "Please, Miss Ruth, what shall we do?" The answer was an airy, "Just evaporate." (Dan Reed, of course, set the ending.)

Her keen awareness of her increasing limitations as a dancer as she got older did not disturb her profoundly. She never forced, she never showed effort, and she worked within her limitations. The platforms for *White Jade* and *The Cobras* got higher and higher as the years passed, since the act of "getting up" was the most difficult problem of all. Just a few years before she died, she quipped, "Leave it to Ruthie to invent getting down on the floor—the ballet dancers were content to be upright but not me—and now I can't get up. So that leaves me with a repertory of exactly six dances, three sitting and three standing!"

The nautch turns slowed down or, rather, she made less revolutions per measure than she once had; the high leg extensions in *Yogi* almost disappeared, but the triumphant stride remained; and in all the old dances, and the new ones too, the glowing spirit of Ruth St. Denis shone forth, and the line of her body and of her gestures remained poems of beauty. In a way, what she did became miniature, instead of expansive, but she never lost perfection.

I tried to help in this way, and the last time I visited with her in 1967, she said, "I am here and I am dancing because of you. Because you were very young and very brash when you first reviewed me—When was it? late thirties?—and because you treated me not like history but like a contemporary dancer. You demanded that of me—no respect for your elders!—and I've tried to deliver the goods ever since."

I always treated her with respect, but I always expected the best from her, for I believed then, and now, that the performer you are watching is on stage *now*, not yesterday, and that although nostalgia is a lovely thing, the echo of song or dance, though softer and gentler, must do honor to its strong origins.

Miss Ruth understood this fully. In 1957 she wrote a poem dedicated to me. In a letter that went with the poem, she took note of the fact that I could not be at Jacob's Pillow, where she first read it to an audience: "Though I was afraid that my great work, my poetic effort entitled: To Dance or not to Dance, dedicated to Walter Terry, would fall quite flat because you were not there, but it didn't!!! So: here it is."

POEM

TO DANCE OR NOT TO DANCE!
When one approaches eighty
one is given to pause.

Of course there is writing to be considered.
There is also acting
which looms up enticingly.
Down the line, well down
There is teaching also to be discussed
with impatient brevity.

To dance or not to
Implies at least the possibility

Miss Ruth

However, the inevitable criticisms,
kindly, not kindly.
constructive, admonishing,
or devastating
hover, as it were, on the horizon.

To dance or not to now . . . ?
Whether it is wiser, to say nothing
Of being easier, to stand and deliver pontifical words,
moving from one side of the stage to the other
with remembered grace,
or to be boldness personified
To the point of the Wagnerian Ego which lifts up
its chin and proclaims to the echoing studio,
"What do you mean? Of course, I shall dance!"

Miss Ruth, of course, continued to dance for the rest
of her life. Exactly ten years later, she put on "the war
paint" just for me and danced "with remembered grace"
in her sun-brushed patio. She was wearing a filmy,
saffron-colored, sarilike shift. The sun was setting, she
tossed her white hair back, and with an ineffably lovely
gesture, she reached out toward those great hills she
loved so well.

Only three years before, she had danced, in a brand
new duet with her husband for the last time. The occasion was the Golden Wedding Anniversary of Ruth St.
Denis and Ted Shawn. Messages poured in from all
over the world, and young dancers, old dancers, old
friends, and new friends flocked to Jacob's Pillow for the

party. On stage, Miss Ruth once again danced *The Incense,* which had turned a divinity student into a dancer and, finally, her husband. Papa Denishawn, or Papa Shawn, as he came to be known by legions of dancers, performed his *St. Francis.* The new duet, based on a poem by Miss Ruth and with a score especially composed by Jess Meeker, was called *Siddhas of the Upper Air.* In the dance itself, they climbed, in close bodily proximity, up a ramp which indicated a new spiritual plane of serenity, of understanding, of revelation.

Miss Ruth and Shawn were truly such landmarks that two years later, in 1966, *National Geographic* celebrated its own fiftieth anniversary of its first use of color by reproducing its first color plate. The subject? Ruth St. Denis and Ted Shawn. In 1916, they were identified only as East Indian dancers, but in the several later reproductions, they were properly named. In 1966, the original color plate and the new *Siddhas* in a color print marked an era for the *Geographic* too.

After the Golden Wedding, in the four years left to her, she remained constantly active. With William Skipper she continued work on her biography on film, an immensely important project, still in progress, relating her dances to her life, to her very being. Skipper, in addition to his work as producer of this project, produced the film of the four great solos, and also a record, called *Ruth St. Denis, First Lady of the American Dance in a "Poetic Biography."* Here is Miss Ruth speaking through her own poetry.

She was also busily at work on the theme of "Rhythms of the Resurrection" and with a plan to organize a dancing choir with women past fifty. In outline was a television series based on the Psalms, which would use the voice of a cantor and three dancing choirs: children, youths, the mature. And then there was to be her series, "Evenings With The Prophets," a multiple-religions evocation of wisdom and guidance from all messengers from God.

At ninety, these were her plans. And, wildly enough, Las Vegas too. Both were Ruth St. Denis. And then she died.

It was a quick and painless passing. She had appeared on TV. The heart began to give way. She was taken to a hospital and, of course, ordered everyone about, sent for her eye make-up, and caused general havoc. A stroke followed, but she never knew that the dancing body could no longer move. She went instantly into that final nap.

She died July 21, 1968, and the newspapers of the world carried the story in full, many on their front pages —the headlines were still hers.

In arranging for services, Shawn and Brother suggested that music from her dances be played by the organist. He couldn't find the appropriate excerpt from *Lakmé,* so, in all innocence, suggested the most convenient ballet music available to him at short notice, *Swan Lake!* Mr. Shawn pierced him with a cold, sharp eye and said, in essence, "If you *dare* use that, my wife will come back and haunt you forever!"

To the last, she was irrepressible. When specialists were gathered about her hospital bed and asked her to stick out her tongue, she snapped: "Which of you four distinguished gentlemen should I stick my tongue out *at?*"

On her tombstone you will read all but the last line of the first poem, "Calling," in her book, *Lotus Light*, first published in 1932:

The Gods have meant
That I should dance,
And by the Gods
I will!
For in some mystic hour
I shall move to unheard rhythms
Of the cosmic orchestra of heaven,
And You will know the language of my wordless songs,
And will come to me——

The final, omitted line, no longer pertinent after ninety-one years, read:
"For that is why I dance."

AN EPILOGUE

The Wit and Wisdom of Ruth St. Denis

WHEN Miss Ruth came to the end of her "more living life," there were tears in the eyes of all who loved her. But one does not mourn for Miss Ruth. One celebrates her. She would have been irked by any other response. And the responses to her husband, to her brother, to me as a dance writer were truly "living" memories. Some were memories of the legend she created. Some were memories of laughter.

Vocha Fiske, as a girl in her teens, saw Miss Ruth dance in Boston in 1909 following the triumphant 1906–09 European tour. Sixty years later, the memory of St. Denis's performance was brightly clear in Miss Fiske's mind. "The house lights dimmed, an insistent drum-beat took over, accompanied by piping flute-like notes, and a single figure dominated and filled the large stage for an hour and a half. These recollections, locked in the 'tablets of memory,' are being set down after fifty years. Yet so profound were their impressions that three images continue fresh, alive. *The Nautch, The Yogi, Radha.* Curiously, color, as well as line, is associated with each. *Nautch,* the dance of professional East Indian dancers, has swirls of gold; *The Yogi,* austere browns; *Radha,* beautiful blues in which rose mingles. . . .

"*The Yogi* now holds center stage. Its browns blend with those of a backdrop whose large old trees interlace in a still, vast, and brooding forest. One feels the silence, the great inner silence of the Yogi at one with it. It radiates to the house until the entire audience, too, feels the hush, awe, reverence in joining with high reality. . . . One embarks with the dancer on a timeless moment of the Unknown. . . ." Miss Fiske's memories of the other dances are equally sharp and immediate. In 1917, when she was a young adult, she wrote a story on Denishawn, the first dance theater in America, for an arts magazine; in 1925, Miss Ruth wrote to the "Chronicler," as she called Miss Fiske, saying, "We are all pilgrims, seekers, learners—of what? of the white flame that burns within, timeless, spaceless, perfect, eternal. This we seek in the *circumference* when it is only to be found in the *center.*"

I have many memories of *The Yogi* myself, all of them memorable, including one that was only one-third there. Miss Ruth was dancing at Jacob's Pillow, and at a certain matinee she strode on, circled the stage, and strode off. The entire center section, the yogi meditation, was omitted along with the finale which repeated the entrance pattern. Miss Ruth was then in her eighties. The staff nurse was sent backstage to the dressing room to see if all was well. There were even some that thought, "This is it. She's gone forever." When the nurse reached the dressing room, she blurted out, "Are you all right, Miss Ruth?" The star answered, "Of course. What made you think I wasn't?" The subject was dropped. But at dinner that night, she said to her husband, "Teddy, it just passes my mind that perhaps I owe you half a dance!"

*   *   *

At ninety, she said to me, "we need balanced government. By that, I mean a man *and* a woman in the White House as a *single* president. First, of course, we need educational facilties to train the woman for a job as the female half of the presidency. There should be an adjacent college, next to the regular college, where women could put in four years of education in government so that they know what government in the United States is all about—trade, banking, etc., but more important, solid training in every aspect of government.

"The women of the world could stop the wars of the world tomorrow. Let's say a boy of five is fighting with the boy next door. Mother restores order. Daddy comes home and wants to know who won. Pride, with the male, comes first. But I don't blame him for his long-held instinct—women are to blame for letting men make a madhouse out of this Earth!"

*   *   *

Miss Ruth

"We're all en*tombed* in our *life*time by ignorance."

*   *   *

In 1960, Miss Ruth on a test for a tape said, "Let me give you this old bromide: I really and truly don't expect to live forever, but, at the moment, all the signs point to the contrary."

*   *   *

In reminiscing about her Delsarte training as a child, she said, "I remember holding on to the old brass bedstead and swinging my legs, lying down on the floor and relaxing, and being told that my emotions were in the middle of me, and that my physical impulses were from the hips down—we won't take time to go into *that* right now—and that from the shoulders up, *all* was spiritual!"

*   *   *

On responding to music as a dancer: "There are three constants to any piece of music. The first is the rhythm. Get to know what the rhythm is about. Let's sit and listen to it; let's count it, let's clap, let's pound it, let's do anything until we've got that rhythm thoroughly in our bones; then the next thing is the melody, naturally. What is that melody? is it short and dramatic? or is it a flowing melody? Let's get that in our minds. Then comes the next thing, the third thing, the dynamics of a piece of music. Where do the *big* dynamics come? Where is it lyrical? Where is it quiet? And then, how many climaxes are there in a piece of music? What almost all amateurs do, if there are one or more climaxes before the *end* climax, they give everything they've got and have nothing left at the end! So my mother always said—and she knew nothing about dancing, but she had a sense of proportion—she said 'Ruthie, that's your best step, keep it.' "

*   *   *

Fifty years after *Egypta,* Miss Ruth said, "What happened to me with *Egypta?* Like a blind kitten I am only beginning to bob around to where does dance come from? And may I give you my definition of dance? with the accent on *my,* meaning that I do not offer it as *the* definition of dance. Dance is the impulse of spirit to move rhythmically, proportionately and perpetually. Now the two words 'rhythmically' and 'perpetually' are understood by most people very readily. The reason I put the word 'proportionately' there I can explain only this way—the vibration of life takes six weeks to bring the seed of a tulip to full flower; it takes two hundred years to do the same thing to the oak tree; it takes a *proportionate* vibration, rhythm, or whatever scientific words you want to use, to bring the tulip to full growth and another proportion to bring the oak tree to full flower. Now that is what I mean by the word 'proportion' and that is that you don't use the same vibration for everything in the universe. A fuchsia takes what? two weeks to grow? But anyway take a little delicate flower that opens before your eyes and in two days is gone. The *proportion* of the *rhythm* which determines the creation of *that* flower maybe comes down to a matter of a few hours, like the life of a butterfly, and then, on the other hand, go to the Yosemite where they have the oldest thing on earth—they tell us—the sequoia trees. Have I made my point?"

*　　*　　*

In 1964, when asked about the gesture she always used —palms held together by the breast as she bowed—for her curtain calls on East Indian dances, she said, "That means a very beautiful thing to the Hindu: it means 'I salute the God in you.' Where we got this pump-handle system of greeting I do not know! I like the Oriental way. I'm a little averse to physical touch with strangers. With the Chinese you put your two hands in your sleeve, clasp them and bow. With the Japanese you put your palms on your thighs and bow. But in no case do you touch the person you are saluting." The interviewer noted that Miss Ruth was wearing white gloves, as a lady should, but wondered if the reason was that she didn't want to touch anyone. "No," she said, "the reason is, darling, that my nail polish is all off."

*　　*　　*

1964—"Our dancers are helping to keep the peace of the world, for whenever you dance you are not under the slavery of our automatic age. Our age is in the hands of scientific prima donnas: they must get to the moon, so that *they* may get the publicity of being first, with the Russians in mind . . . [nor do] we care, *par exemple*, about reforming our educational system, which is ALL WET." And I think it wise to say here and now that Miss Ruth, a radical in the arts, was a very conservative Republican.

*   *   *

In commenting on the radical change which took place in women's dress because of her Hindu costume, she described the process: "My costume, in *Incense*, consists of a sari which today the women of America are fairly familiar with. Then we have what we call a choli, which is a little jacket, and this little jacket covers the shoulders, the bust, and the upper part of the diaphragm and then . . . it rests a while! And then comes the skirt which leaves epidermis—is that the word you scholars would use?—it leaves about three inches of epidermis. So this did startle the ladies of 1900 and intrigued the gentlemen. So that in no time flat we had an imitation of my *Incense* costume done with all kinds of colors but with the three inches of epidermis. Very soon, just how, I don't know, it got into what we coyly call 'underthings,' or lingerie if you want to be grand about it. So today we have bras and panties, and I was the grandmother, or great grandmother, of all this." (Taped interview, 1964.)

*   *   *

Interviewed after the fiftieth wedding anniversary celebrations for herself and Ted Shawn, when asked about the various possibilities attendant upon her age, she said,

"I honestly and truly don't know how old I am—probably somewhere between eight-four and eighty-seven. I did find an old passport from my Belasco days not long ago, but I don't know what I have done with it. Too bad, because *it* told the truth! So let us say today that the best way to pinpoint my age is to admit that it works, dears, on a *sliding* scale!"

*   *   *

1964 taping—"As I watch this field of dancers whirling around and around, this thought came to mind—and Walter and I are going to do an essay on it—that it is the business of the American dance at its most powerful and most esthetic dimensions to help change the fashions of America, which at this moment I think are Godawful! Have you been in a New York subway lately? Well, I have. Opposite, at rush hour, comes a rather heavy-set lady, who has paid all of two dollars for the latest skirt. She sits down and she's tired. You get her kneecaps to start with . . . well, I'M a lady, I can't go on!"

*   *   *

On tape, at 87—"I believe that all creative minds in every field of the arts—painting, poetry, sculpture, and the rest—live, take them by and large, a more living life than other people."

*   *   *

"Fifty years married to the same man. Get that!"

*   *   *

Reacting to a young dancer who relied solely on technique: "He showed us what he had learned in four or five years. He went on and on. He showed us that he could hold that right leg up there until you just groaned. *He* didn't groan—*he* was all right—but *you* did. I couldn't take it. To me it was the utter desecration of dance. He simply came out of the classroom and showed us what he could do, DO! DO! And it didn't mean a damn thing."

*   *   *

Of her own brief period of lessons in ballet with Mme Bonfanti, she recalled: "I was the clumsiest thing as a ballet dancer that you have ever seen. And I asked inconvenient questions. I was altogether an unsatisfactory pupil. No wonder she suggested that I seek classes elsewhere!"

*   *   *

"The dance begins in consciousness, not in the body."

*   *   *

"Isadora belongs to the Dionysiac school. Under the impact of music or by her own inner ecstasy, *she* danced without much pattern but with such perfect co-ordination of beauty and body. *I* am a born ritualist."

*   *   *

In 1963, in her dressing room, she looked at her bare midriff in the mirror and said, "I've still got the torso.

So maybe the audience would be wise not to look above it or below it, but to concentrate on my middle!"

*　　*　　*

Of Isadora, "she offered herself. She exalted the human being while she was dancing."

*　　*　　*

Of herself, she wrote:

MAJESTY OF THE LOTUS

I have a line, a destiny, a plan that I must follow.
My soul beheld itself in majesty
In Egypt, in India, in Syria, in China.
Always in majesty . . . in power . . . in stillness.
This was the form, the design
That was given me at the beginning.
It is now and ever will be with me.
So at the beginning I lift up my eyes to the throne.
That which is 'past' is forever present,
And I lift up my spirit to behold the 'future'
Which is also in the forever present.

The thread runs through the beads of time,
The image does not change.
It is ever white,
It is ever royal,
It is ever still.
It is the heart and seed place of the Lotus.

R. St. D.

INDEX

Index